MILITARY HISTORY
FROM PRIMARY SOURCES

TRIBES OF ANCIENT BRITAIN AND GERMANY

EDITED AND INTRODUCED
BY BOB CARRUTHERS

C⊕DA
BOOKS LTD
www.codabooks.com

This edition published in Great Britain in 2012 by

Coda Books Ltd, The Barn, Cutlers Farm Business Centre, Edstone,

Wootton Wawen, Henley in Arden, Warwickshire, B95 6DJ

www.codabooks.com

C⊕DA
BOOKS LTD

Copyright © 2012 Coda Books Ltd.

A CIP catalogue record for this book is available from the British Library.

ISBN: 978-1-78158-152-0

CONTENTS

AN INTRODUCTION
TO THE AUTHOR

P UBLIUS (OR GAIUS) Cornelius Tacitus (AD 56 – AD 117) was a senator and a historian of the Roman Empire. The surviving portions of his two major works - the Annals and the Histories - examine the reigns of the Roman Emperors Tiberius, Claudius, Nero and those who reigned in the Year of the Four Emperors. These two works span the history of the Roman Empire from the death of Augustus in AD 14 to the death of Emperor Domitian in AD 96. There are substantial lacunae in the surviving texts, including one four books long in the Annals.

Other writings by him discuss oratory (in dialogue format, see Dialogus de oratoribus), Germania (in De origine et situ Germanorum), and the life of his father-in-law Agricola, mainly focusing on his campaign in Britannia (see De vita et moribus Iulii Agricolae).

Tacitus is considered one of the greatest Roman historians, living in what has been called the Silver Age of Latin literature. As well as the brevity and compactness of his Latin prose, he is known for his penetrating insights into the psychology of power politics.

Details about his personal life are scarce. What little is known comes from scattered hints throughout his work, the letters of his friend and admirer Pliny the Younger, and an inscription found at Mylasa in Caria.

Tacitus was born in 56 or 57 to an equestrian family; like many Latin authors of both the Golden and Silver Ages, he was from the provinces, probably in northern Italy or Gallia Narbonensis. The exact place and date of his birth are not known, and his praenomen (first name) is also unknown; in the letters of Sidonius Apollinaris his name is Gaius, but in the major surviving manuscript of his work his name is given as Publius. One scholar's suggestion of Sextus has gained no traction.

FAMILY AND EARLY LIFE

Most of the older aristocratic families failed to survive the proscriptions which took place at the end of the Republic, and Tacitus makes it clear that he owes his rank to the Flavian emperors (Hist. 1.1). The claim that he descended from a freedman derives from a speech in his writings that asserts that many senators and knights were descended from freedmen (Ann. 13.27), but this is generally disputed.

His father may have been the Cornelius Tacitus who was procurator of Belgica and Germania; Pliny the Elder mentions that Cornelius had a son who grew and aged rapidly (N.H. 7.76), which implies an early death. If Cornelius was his father, and since there is no mention of Tacitus suffering such a condition, it is possible that this refers to a brother. The friendship between the younger Pliny and Tacitus leads some scholars to conclude that they were both the offspring of wealthy provincial families.

Although the province of his birth is unknown (and has been variously conjectured as Gallia Belgica, Gallia Narbonensis, or northern Italy) his marriage to the daughter of the Narbonensian senator Gnaeus Julius Agricola implies that he came from Gallia Narbonensis. Tacitus' dedication to Fabius Iustus in the Dialogus may indicate a connection with Spain, and his friendship with Pliny suggests that he was born in northern Italy. No evidence exists however that Pliny's friends from northern Italy knew Tacitus, nor do Pliny's letters hint that the two men had a common background. Pliny Book 9, Letter 23 reports that when he was asked if he was Italian or provincial, he gave an unclear answer, and so was asked if he was Tacitus or Pliny. Since Pliny was from Italy, some infer that Tacitus was from the provinces, probably Gallia Narbonensis.

His ancestry, his skill in oratory, and his sympathetic depiction of barbarians who resisted Roman rule (e.g., Ann. 2.9), have led to suggestions that he was a Celt. This belief stems from the fact that

that the Celts occupied Gaul prior to the Roman invasion and were famous for their skill in oratory, and had been subjugated by Rome.

PUBLIC LIFE, MARRIAGE, AND LITERARY CAREER

As a young man, Tacitus studied rhetoric in Rome to prepare for a career in law and politics; like Pliny, he may have studied under Quintilian. In 77 or 78 he married , daughter of the famous general Agricola; although little is known of their home life, save that Tacitus loved and the outdoors. He started his career (probably the latus clavus, mark of the senator) under Vespasian, but it was in 81 or 82, under Titus, that he entered political life, as quaestor. He advanced steadily through the cursus honorum, becoming praetor in 88 and a quindecimvir, a member of the priest college in charge of the Sibylline Books and the Secular games. He gained acclaim as a lawyer and an orator; his skill in public speaking is ironic given his cognomen: Tacitus ("silent").

He served in the provinces from ca. 89 to ca. 93 either in command of a legion or in a civilian post. He (and his property) survived Domitian's reign of terror (81–96), but the experience left him jaded and perhaps ashamed at his own complicity, giving him the hatred of tyranny which is so evident in his works. The Agricola, chs. 44–45, is illustrative:

Agricola was spared those later years during which Domitian, leaving now no interval or breathing space of time, but, as it were, with one continuous blow, drained the life-blood of the Commonwealth... It was not long before our hands dragged Helvidius to prison, before we gazed on the dying looks of Manricus and Rusticus, before we were steeped in Senecio's innocent blood. Even Nero turned his eyes away, and did not gaze upon the atrocities which he ordered; with Domitian it was the chief part of our miseries to see and to be seen, to know that our sighs were being recorded.

From his seat in the Senate he became suffect consul in 97 during the reign of Nerva, being the first of his family to do so. During his tenure he reached the height of his fame as an orator when he delivered the funeral oration for the famous veteran soldier Lucius Verginius Rufus.

In the following year he wrote and published the Agricola and Germania, announcing the beginnings of the literary endeavors that would occupy him until his death. Afterwards he absented himself from public life, but returned during Trajan's reign. In 100, he, along with his friend Pliny the Younger, prosecuted Marius Priscus (proconsul of Africa) for corruption. Priscus was found guilty and sent into exile; Pliny wrote a few days later that Tacitus had spoken "with all the majesty which characterizes his usual style of oratory".

A lengthy absence from politics and law followed while he wrote the Histories and the Annals. In 112 or 113 he held the highest civilian governorship, that of the Roman province of Asia in Western Anatolia, recorded in the inscription found at Mylasa mentioned above. A passage in the Annals fixes 116 as the terminus post quem of his death, which may have been as late as 125 or even 130. It seems that he survived both Pliny and Trajan. It is unknown whether he had any children, because although the Augustan History reports that the emperor Marcus Claudius Tacitus claimed him for an ancestor and provided for the preservation of his works, like much of the Augustan History, this story may be fraudulent.

TRIBES OF ANCIENT BRITAIN

1. To bequeath to posterity a record of the deeds and characters of distinguished men is an ancient practice which even the present age, careless as it is of its own sons, has not abandoned whenever some great and conspicuous excellence has conquered and risen superior to that failing, common to petty and to great states, blindness and hostility to goodness. But in days gone by, as there was a greater inclination and a more open path to the achievement of memorable actions, so the man of highest genius was led by the simple reward of a good conscience to hand on without partiality or self-seeking the remembrance of greatness. Many too thought that to write their own lives showed the confidence of integrity rather than presumption. Of Rutilius and Scaurus no one doubted the honesty or questioned the motives. So true is it that merit is best appreciated by the age in which it thrives most easily. But in these days, I, who have to record the life of one who has passed away, must crave an indulgence, which I should not have had to ask had I an indulgence, which I should not have had to ask had I only to inveigh against an age so cruel, so hostile to all virtue.

2. We have only to read that the panegyrics pronounced by Arulenus Rusticus on Paetus Thrasea, and by Herennius Senecio on Priscus Helvidius, were made capital crimes, that not only their persons but their very books were objects of rage, and that the triumvirs were commissioned to burn in the forum those works of splendid genius. They fancied, forsooth, that in that fire the voice of the Roman people, the freedom of the Senate, and the conscience of the human race were perishing, while at the same time they banished the teachers of philosophy, and exiled every noble pursuit, that nothing good might anywhere confront them. Certainly we showed a magnificent example of patience; as a former age had witnessed the extreme of liberty, so we witnessed the extreme of servitude, when the informer robbed us of the

interchanges of speech, and hearing. We should have lost memory as well as voice, had it been as easy to forget as to keep silence.

3. Now at last our spirit is returning. And yet, though at the dawn of a most happy age Nerva Caesar blended things once irreconcilable, sovereignty and freedom; though Nerva Trajan is now daily augmenting the prosperity of the time, and though the public safety has not only our hopes and good wishes, but has also the certain pledge of their fulfillment: still, from the necessary condition of human frailty, the remedy works less quickly than the disease. As our bodies grow but slowly, perish in a moment, so it is easier to crush than to revive genius and its pursuits. Besides, the charm of indolence steals over us, and the idleness which at first we loathed we afterwards love. What if during those fifteen years, a large portion of human life, many were cut off by ordinary casualties, and the ablest fell victim to the Emperor's rage, if a few of us survive, though there have been taken from the midst of life those many years which brought the young in dumb silence to old age, and the old almost to the very verge and end of existence! Yet we shall not regret that we have told, though in language unskilful and unadorned, the story of past servitude, and borne our testimony to present happiness. Meanwhile this book, intended to do honour to Agricola, my father-in-law, will, as an expression of filial regard, be commended, or at least excused.

4. Cnaeus Julius Agricola was born at the ancient and famous colony of Forum Julii. Each of his grandfathers was an Imperial procurator, that is, of the highest equestrian rank. His father, Julius Graecinus, a member of the Senatorian order, and distinguished for his pursuit of eloquence and philosophy, earned for himself by these very merits the displeasure of Caius Caesar. He was ordered to impeach Marcus Silanus, and because he refused was put to death. His mother was Julia Procilla, a lady of singular virtue. Brought up by her side with fond affection, he passed his boyhood and youth in the cultivation of every worthy attainment. He was guarded from the enticements of the profligate not only by his own

good and straight- forward character, but also by having, when quite a child, for the scene and guide of his studies, Massilia, a place where refinement and provincial frugality were blended and happily combined. I remember that he used to tell us how in his early youth he would have imbibed a keener love of philosophy than became a Roman and a senator, had not his mother's good sense checked his excited and ardent spirit. It was the case of a lofty and aspiring soul craving with more eagerness than caution the beauty and splendour of great and glorious renown. But it was soon mellowed by reason and experience, and he retained from his learning that most difficult of lessons - moderation.

5. He served his military apprenticeship in Britain to the satisfaction of Suetonius Paullinus, a painstaking and judicious officer, who, to test his merits, selected him to share his tent. Without the recklessness with which young men often make the profession of arms a mere pastime, and without indolence, he never availed himself of his tribune's rank or his inexperience to procure enjoyment or to escape from duty. He sought to make himself acquainted with the province and known to the army; he would learn from the skilful, and keep pace with the bravest, would attempt nothing for display, would avoid nothing from fear, and would be at once careful and vigilant. Never indeed had Britain been more excited, or in a more critical condition. Veteran soldiers had been massacred, colonies burnt, armies cut off. The struggle was then for safety; it was soon to be for victory. And though all this was conducted under the leadership and direction of another, though the final issue and the glory of having won back the province belonged to the general, yet skill, experience, and ambition were acquired by the young officer. His soul too was penetrated with the desire of warlike renown, a sentiment unwelcome to an age which put a sinister construction on eminent merit, and made glory as perilous as infamy.

6. From Britain he went to Rome, to go through the regular course of office, and there allied himself with Domitia Decidiana,

a lady of illustrious birth. The marriage was one which gave a man ambitious of advancement distinction and support. They lived in singular harmony, through their mutual affection and preference of each other to self. However, the good wife deserves the greater praise, just as the bad incurs a heavier censure. Appointed Quaestor, the ballot gave him Asia for his province, Salvius Titianus for his proconsul. Neither the one nor the other corrupted him, though the province was rich and an easy prey to the wrongdoer, while the proconsul, a man inclined to every species of greed, was ready by all manner of indulgence to purchase a mutual concealment of guilt. A daughter was there added to his family to be his stay and comfort, for shortly after he lost the son that had before been born to him. The year between his quaestorship and tribunate, as well as the year of the tribunate itself, he passed in retirement and inaction, for he knew those times of Nero when indolence stood for wisdom. His praetorship was passed in the same consistent quietude, for the usual judicial functions did not fall to his lot. The games and the pageantry of his office he ordered according to the mean between strictness and profusion, avoiding extravagance, but not missing distinction. He was afterwards appointed by Galba to draw up an account of the temple offerings, and his searching scrutiny relieved the conscience of the stte from the burden of all sacrileges but those committed by Nero.

7. The following year inflicted a terrible blow on his affections and his fortunes. Otho's fleet, while cruising idly about, cruelly ravaged Intemelii, a district of Liguria; his mother, who was living here on her own estate, was murdered. The estate itself and a large part of her patrimony were plundered. This was indeed the occasion of the crime. Agricola, who instantly set out to discharge the duties of affection, was overtaken by the tidings that Vespasian was aiming at the throne. He at once joined his party. Vespasian's early policy, and the government of Rome were directed by Mucianus, for Domitian was a mere youth, and from his father's elevation sought only the opportunities of indulgence. Agricola,

having been sent by Mucianus to conduct a levy of troops, and having done his work with integrity and energy, was appointed to command the 20th Legion, which had been slow to take the new oath of allegiance, and the retiring officer of which was reported to be acting disloyally. It was a trying and formidable charge for even officers of consular rank, and the late praetorian officer, perhaps from his own disposition, perhaps from that of the soldiers, was powerless to restrain them. Chosen thus at once to supersede and to punish, Agricola, with a singular moderation, wished it to be thought that he had found rather than made an obedient soldiery.

8. Britain was then under Vettius Bolanus, who governed more mildly than suited so turbulent a province. Agricola moderated his energy and restrained his ardour, that he might not grow too important, for he had learnt to obey, and understood well how to combine expediency with honour. Soon afterwards Britain received for its governor a man of consular rank, Petilius Cerialis. Agricola's merits had now room for display. Cerialis let him share at first indeed only the toils and dangers, but before long the glory of war, often by way of trial putting him in command of part of the army, and sometimes, on the strength of the result, of larger forces. Never to enhance his own renown did Agricola boast of his exploits; he always referred his success, as though he were but an instrument, to his general and director. Thus by his valour in obeying orders and by his modesty of speech he escaped jealousy without losing distinction.

9. As he was returning from the command of the legion, Vespasian admitted him into the patrician order, and then gave him the province of Aquitania, a preeminently splendid appointment both from the importance of its duties and the prospect of the consulate to which the Emperor destined him. Many think the genius of the soldier wants subtlety, because military law, which is summary and blunt, and apt to appeal to the sword, finds no exercise for the refinements of the forum. Yet Agricola, from his natural good sense, though called to act among civilians, did his

work with ease and correctness. And, besides, the times of business and relaxation were kept distinct. When his public and judicial duties required it, he was dignified, thoughtful, austere, and yet often merciful; when business was done with, he wore no longer the official character. He was altogether without harshness, pride, or the greed of gain. With a most rare felicity, his good nature did not weaken his authority, nor his strictness the attachment of his friends. To speak of uprightness and purity in such a man would be an insult to his virtues. Fame itself, of which even good men are often weakly fond, he did not seek by an ostentation of virtue or by artifice. He avoided rivalry with his colleagues, contention with his procurator, thinking such victories no honour and defeat disgrace. For somewhat less than three years he was kept in his governorship, and was then recalled with an immediate prospect of the consulate. A general belief went with him that the province of Britain was to be his, not because he had himself hinted it, but because he seemed worthy of it. Public opinion is not always mistaken; sometimes even it chooses the right man. He was consul, and I but a youth, when he betrothed to me his daughter, a maiden even then of noble promise. After his consulate he gave her to me in marriage, and was then at once appointed to the government of Britain, with the addition of the sacred office of the pontificate.

10. The geography and inhabitants of Britain, already described by so many writers, I will speak of, not that my research and ability may be compared with theirs, but because the country was then for the first time thoroughly subdued. And so matters, which as being still not accurately known my predecessors embellished with their eloquence, shall now be related on the evidence of facts. Britain, the largest of the islands which Roman geography includes, is so situated that it faces Germany on the east, Spain on the west; on the south it is even within sight of Gaul; its northern extremities, which have no shores opposite to them, are beaten by the waves of a vast open sea. The form of the entire country has been compared by Livy and Fabius Rusticus, the most graphic among ancient and

modern historians, to an oblong shield or battle-axe. And this no doubt is its shape without Caledonia, so that it has become the popular description of the whole island. There is, however, a large and irregular tract of land which juts out from its furthest shores, tapering off in a wedge-like form. Round these coasts of remotest ocean the Roman fleet then for the first time sailed, ascertained that Britain is an island, and simultaneously discovered and conquered what are called the Orcades, islands hitherto unknown. Thule too was descried in the distance, which as yet had been hidden by the snows of winter. Those waters, they say, are sluggish, and yield with difficulty to the oar, and are not even raised by the wind as other seas. The reason, I suppose, is that lands and mountains, which are the cause and origin of storms, are here comparatively rare, and also that the vast depths of that unbroken expanse are more slowly set in motion. But to investigate the nature of the ocean and the tides is no part of the present work, and many writers have discussed the subject. I would simply add, that nowhere has the sea a wider dominion, that it has many currents running in every direction, that it does not merely flow and ebb within the limits of the shore, but penetrates and winds far inland, and finds a home among hills and mountains as though in its own domain.

11. Who were the original inhabitants of Britain, whether they were indigenous or foreign, is as usual among barbarians, little known. Their physical characteristics are various, and from these conclusions may be drawn. The red hair and large limbs of the inhabitants of Caledonia point clearly to a German origin. The dark complexion of the Silures, their usually curly hair, and the fact that Spain is the opposite shore to them, are an evidence that Iberians of a former date crossed over and occupied these parts. Those who are nearest to the Gauls are also like them, either from the permanent influence of original descent, or, because in countries which run out so far to meet each other, climate has produced similar physical qualities. But a general survey inclines me to believe that the Gauls established themselves in an island so

near to them. Their religious belief may be traced in the strongly-marked British superstition. The language differs but little; there is the same boldness in challenging danger, and, when it is near, the same timidity in shrinking from it. The Britons, however, exhibit more spirit, as being a people whom a long peace has not yet enervated. Indeed we have understood that even the Gauls were once renowned in war; but, after a while, sloth following on ease crept over them, and they lost their courage along with their freedom. This too has happened to the long-conquered tribes of Britain; the rest are still what the Gauls once were.

12. Their strength is in infantry. Some tribes fight also with the chariot. The higher in rank is the charioteer; the dependants fight. They were once ruled by kings, but are now divided under chieftains into factions and parties. Our greatest advantage in coping with tribes so powerful is that they do not act in concert. Seldom is it that two or three states meet together to ward off a common danger. Thus, while they fight singly, all are conquered. Their sky is obscured by continual rain and cloud. Severity of cold is unknown. The days exceed in length those of our part of the world; the nights are bright, and in the extreme north so short that between sunlight and dawn you can perceive but a slight distinction. It is said that, if there are no clouds in the way, the splendour of the sun can be seen throughout the night, and that he does not rise and set, but only crosses the heavens. The truth is, that the low shadow thrown from the flat extremities of the earth's surface does not raise the darkness to any height, and the night thus fails to reach the sky and stars. With the exception of the olive and vine, and plants which usually grow in warmer climates, the soil will yield, and even abundantly, all ordinary produce. It ripens indeed slowly, but is of rapid growth, the cause in each case being the same, namely, the excessive moisture of the soil and of the atmosphere. Britain contains gold and silver and other metals, as the prize of conquest. The ocean, too, produces pearls, but of a dusky and bluish hue. Some think that those who collect

them have not the requisite skill, as in the Red Sea the living and breathing pearl is torn from the rocks, while in Britain they are gathered just as they are thrown up. I could myself more readily believe that the natural properties of the pearls are in fault than our keenness for gain.

13. The Britons themselves bear cheerfully the conscription, the taxes, and the other burdens imposed on them by the Empire, if there be no oppression. Of this they are impatient; they are reduced to subjection, not as yet to slavery. The deified Julius, the very first Roman who entered Britain with an army, though by a successful engagement he struck terror into the inhabitants and gained possession of the coast, must be regarded as having indicated rather than transmitted the acquisition to future generations. Then came the civil wars, and the arms of our leaders were turned against their country, and even when there was peace, there was a long neglect of Britain. This Augustus spoke of as policy, Tiberius as an inherited maxim. That Caius Caesar meditated an invasion of Britain is perfectly clear, but his purposes, rapidly formed, were easily changed, and his vast attempts on Germany had failed. Claudius was the first to renew the attempt, and conveyed over into the island some legions and auxiliaries, choosing Vespasian to share with him the campaign, whose approaching elevation had this beginning. Several tribes were subdued and kings made prisoners, and destiny learnt to know its favourite.

14. Aulus Plautius was the first governor of consular rank, and Ostorius Scapula the next. Both were famous soldiers, and by degrees the nearest portions of Britain were brought into the condition of a province, and a colony of veterans was also introduced. Some of the states were given to king Cogidumnus, who lived down to our day a most faithful ally. So was maintained the ancient and long-recognised practice of the Roman people, which seeks to secure among the instruments of dominion even kings themselves. Soon after, Didius Gallus consolidated the conquests of his predecessors, and advanced a very few positions

into parts more remote, to gain the credit of having enlarged the sphere of government. Didius was succeeded by Veranius, who died within the year. Then Suetonius Paullinus enjoyed success for two years; he subdued several tribes and strengthened our military posts. Thus encouraged, he made an attempt on the island of Mona, as a place from which the rebels drew reinforcements; but in doing this he left his rear open to attack.

15. Relieved from apprehension by the legate's absence, the Britons dwelt much among themselves on the miseries of subjection, compared their wrongs, and exaggerated them in the discussion. "All we get by patience," they said, "is that heavier demands are exacted from us, as from men who will readily submit. A single king once ruled us; now two are set over us; a legate to tyrannise over our lives, a procurator to tyrannise over our property. Their quarrels and their harmony are alike ruinous to their subjects. The centurions of the one, the slaves of the other, combine violence with insult. Nothing is now safe from their avarice, nothing from their lust. In war it is the strong who plunders; now, it is for the most part by cowards and poltroons that our homes are rifled, our children torn from us, the conscription enforced, as though it were for our country alone that we could not die. For, after all, what a mere handful of soldiers has crossed over, if we Britons look at our own numbers. Germany did thus shake off the yoke, and yet its defence was a river, not the ocean. With us, fatherland, wives, parents, are the motives to war; with them, only greed and profligacy. They will surely fly, as did the now deified Julius, if once we emulate the valour of our sires. Let us not be panic-stricken at the result of one or two engagements. The miserable have more fury and greater resolution. Now even the gods are beginning to pity us, for they are keeping away the Roman general, and detaining his army far from us in another island. We have already taken the hardest step; we are deliberating. And indeed, in all such designs, to dare is less perilous than to be detected."

16. Rousing each other by this and like language, under the leadership of Boudicea, a woman of kingly descent (for they admit no distinction of sex in their royal successions), they all rose in arms. They fell upon our troops, which were scattered on garrison duty, stormed the forts, and burst into the colony itself, the head-quarters, as they thought, of tyranny. In their rage and their triumph, they spared no variety of a barbarian's cruelty. Had not Paullinus on hearing of the outbreak in the province rendered prompt succour, Britain would have been lost. By one successful engagement, he brought it back to its former obedience, though many, troubled by the conscious guilt of rebellion and by particular dread of the legate, still clung to their arms. Excellent as he was in other respects, his policy to the conquered was arrogant, and exhibited the cruelty of one who was avenging private wrongs. Accordingly Petronius Turpilianus was sent out to initiate a milder rule. A stranger to the enemy's misdeeds and so more accessible to their penitence, he put an end to old troubles, and, attempting nothing more, handed the province over to Trebellius Maximus. Trebellius, who was somewhat indolent, and never ventured on a campaign, controlled the province by a certain courtesy in his administration. Even the barbarians now learnt to excuse many attractive vices, and the occurrence of the civil war gave a good pretext for inaction. But we were sorely troubled with mutiny, as troops habituated to service grew demoralised by idleness. Trebellius, who had escaped the soldiers' fury by flying and hiding himself, governed henceforth on sufferance, a disgraced and humbled man. It was a kind of bargain; the soldiers had their license, the general had his life; and so the mutiny cost no bloodshed. Nor did Vettius Bolanus, during the continuance of the civil wars, trouble Britain with discipline. There was the same inaction with respect to the enemy, and similar unruliness in the camp, only Bolanus, an upright man, whom no misdeeds made odious, had secured affection in default of the power of control.

17. When however Vespasian had restored to unity Britain as

well as the rest of the world, in the presence of the great generals and renowned armies the enemy's hopes were crushed. They were at once panic-stricken by the attack of Petilius Cerialis on the state of the Brigantes, said to be the most prosperous in the entire province. There were many battles, some by no means bloodless, and his conquests, or at least his wars, embraced a large part of the territory of the Brigantes. Indeed he would have altogether thrown into the shade the activity and renown of any other successor; but Julius Frontus was equal to the burden, a great man as far as greatness was then possible, who subdued by his arms the powerful and warlike tribe of the Silures, surmounting the difficulties of the country as well as the valour of the enemy.

18. Such was the state of Britain, and such were the vicissitudes of the war, which Agricola found on his crossing over about midsummer. Our soldiers made it a pretext for carelessness, as if all fighting was over, and the enemy were biding their time. The Ordovices, shortly before Agricola's arrival, had destroyed nearly the whole of a squadron of allied cavalry quartered in their territory. Such a beginning raised the hopes of the country, and all who wished for war approved the precedent, and anxiously watched the temper of the new governor. Meanwhile Agricola, though summer was past and the detachments were scattered throughout the province, though the soldiers' confident anticipation of inaction for that year would be a source of delay and difficulty in beginning a campaign, and most advisers thought it best simply to watch all weak points, resolved to face the peril. He collected a force of veterans and a small body of auxiliaries; then as the Ordovices would not venture to descend into the plain, he put himself in front of the ranks to inspire all with the same courage against a common danger, and led his troops up a hill. The tribe was all but exterminated. Well aware that he must follow up the prestige of his arms, and that in proportion to his first success would be the terror of the other tribes, he formed the design of subjugating the island of Mona, from the occupation of which Paulinus had been recalled, as I have

already related, by the rebellion of the entire province. But, as his plans were not matured, he had no fleet. The skill and resolution of the general accomplished the passage. With some picked men of the auxiliaries, disencumbered of all baggage, who knew the shallows and had that national experience in swimming which enables the Britons to take care not only of themselves but of their arms and horses, he delivered so unexpected an attack that the astonished enemy who were looking for a fleet, a naval armament, and an assault by sea, thought that to such assailants nothing could be formidable or invincible. And so, peace having been sued for and the island given up, Agricola became great and famous as one who, when entering on his province, a time which others spend in vain display and a round of ceremonies, chose rather toil and danger. Nor did he use his success for self-glorification, or apply the name of campaigns and victories to the repression of a conquered people. He did not even describe his achievements in a laurelled letter. Yet by thus disguising his renown he really increased it, for men inferred the grandeur of his aspirations from his silence about services so great.

19. Next, with thorough insight into the feelings of his province, and taught also, by the experience of others, that little is gained by conquest if followed by oppression, he determined to root out the causes of war. Beginning first with himself and his dependants, he kept his household under restraint, a thing as hard to many as ruling a province. He transacted no public business through freedmen or slaves; no private leanings, no recommendations or entreaties of friends, moved him in the selection of centurions and soldiers, but it was ever the best man whom he thought most trustworthy. He knew everything, but did not always act on his knowledge. Trifling errors he treated with leniency, serious offences with severity. Nor was it always punishment, but far oftener penitence, which satisfied him. He preferred to give office and power to men who would not transgress, rather than have to condemn a transgressor. He lightened the exaction of corn and

tribute by an equal distribution of the burden, while he got rid of those contrivances for gain which were more intolerable than the tribute itself. Hitherto the people had been compelled to endure the farce of waiting by the closed granary and of purchasing corn unnecessarily and raising it to a fictitious price. Difficult byroads and distant places were fixed for them, so that states with a winter-camp close to them had to carry corn to remote and inaccessible parts of the country, until what was within the reach of all became a source of profit to the few.

20. Agricola, by the repression of these abuses in his very first year in office, restored to peace its good name, when, from either the indifference or the harshness of his predecessors, it had come to be as much dreaded as war. When, however, summer came, assembling his forces, he continually showed himself in the ranks, praised good discipline, and kept the stragglers in order. He would himself choose the position of the camp, himself explore the estuaries and forests. Meanwhile he would allow the enemy no rest, laying waste his territory with sudden incursions, and, having sufficiently alarmed him, would then by forbearance display the allurements of peace. In consequence, many states, which up to that time had been in- dependent, gave hostages, and laid aside their animosities; garrisons and forts were established among them with a skill and diligence with which no newly-acquired part of Britain had before been treated.

21. The following winter passed without disturbance, and was employed in salutary measures. For, to accustom to rest and repose through the charms of luxury a population scattered and barbarous and therefore inclined to war, Agricola gave private encouragement and public aid to the building of temples, courts of justice and dwelling-houses, praising the energetic, and reproving the indolent. Thus an honourable rivalry took the place of compulsion. He likewise provided a liberal education for the sons of the chiefs, and showed such a preference for the natural powers of the Britons over the industry of the Gauls that they who

lately disdained the tongue of Rome now coveted its eloquence. Hence, too, a liking sprang up for our style of dress, and the "toga" became fashionable. Step by step they were led to things which dispose to vice, the lounge, the bath, the elegant banquet. All this in their ignorance they called civilisation, when it was but a part of their servitude.

22. The third year of his campaigns opened up new tribes, our ravages on the native population being carried as far as the Taus, an estuary so called. This struck such terror into the enemy that he did not dare to attack our army, harassed though it was by violent storms; and there was even time for the erection of forts. It was noted by experienced officers that no general had ever shown more judgment in choosing suitable positions, and that not a single fort established by Agricola was either stormed by the enemy or abandoned by capitulation or flight. Sorties were continually being made; for these positions were secured from protracted siege by a year's supply. So winter brought with it no alarms, and each garrison could hold its own, as the baffled and despairing enemy, who had been accustomed often to repair his summer losses by winter successes, found himself repelled alike both in summer and winter. Never did Agricola in a greedy spirit appropriate the achievements of others; the centurion and the prefect both found in him an impartial witness of their every action. Some persons used to say that he was too harsh in his reproofs, and that he was as severe to the bad as he was gentle to the good. But his dis- pleasure left nothing behind it; reserve and silence in him were not to be dreaded. He thought it better to show anger than to cherish hatred.

23. The fourth summer he employed in securing what he had overrun. Had the valour of our armies and the renown of the Roman name permitted it, a limit to our conquests might have been found in Britain itself. Clota and Bodotria, estuaries which the tides of two opposite seas carry far back into the country, are separated by but a narrow strip of land. This Agricola then began to defend with a line of forts, and, as all the country to the south

was now occupied, the enemy were pushed into what might be called another island.

24. In the fifth year of the war, Agricola, himself in the leading ship, crossed the Clota, and subdued in a series of victories tribes hitherto unknown. In that part of Britain which looks toward Ireland, he posted some troops, hoping for fresh conquests rather than fearing attack, inasmuch as Ireland, being between Britain and Spain and conveniently situated for the seas round Gaul, might have been the means of connecting with great mutual benefit the most powerful parts of the empire. Its extent is small when compared with Britain, but exceeds the islands of our seas. In soil and climate, in the disposition, temper, and habits of its population, it differs but little from Britain. We know most of its harbours and approaches, and that through the intercourse of commerce. One of the petty kings of the nation, driven out by internal faction, had been received by Agricola, who detained him under the semblance of friendship till he could make use of him. I have often heard him say that a single legion with a few auxiliaries could conquer and occupy Ireland, and that it would have a salutary effect on Britain for the Roman arms to be seen everywhere, and for freedom, so to speak, to be banished from its sight.

25. In the summer in which he entered on the sixth year of his office, his operations embraced the states beyond Bodotria, and, as he dreaded a general movement among the remoter tribes, as well as the perils which would beset an invading army, he explored the harbours with a fleet, which, at first employed by him as an integral part of his force, continued to accompany him. The spectacle of war thus pushed on at once by sea and land was imposing; while often infantry, cavalry, and marines, mingled in the same encampment and joyously sharing the same meals, would dwell on their own achievements and adventures, comparing, with a soldier's boastfulness, at one time the deep recesses of the forest and the mountain with the dangers of waves and storms, or, at another, battles by land with victories over the ocean. The Britons,

too, as we learnt from the prisoners, were confounded by the sight of a fleet, as if, now that their inmost seas were penetrated, the conquered had their last refuge closed to them. The tribes inhabiting Caledonia flew to arms, and with great preparations, made greater by the rumours which always exaggerate the unknown, themselves advanced to attack our fortresses, and thus challenging a conflict, inspired us with alarm. To retreat south of the Bodotria, and to retire rather than to be driven out, was the advice of timid pretenders to prudence, when Agricola learnt that the enemy's attack would be made with more than one army. Fearing that their superior numbers and their knowledge of the country might enable them to hem him in, he too distributed his forces into three divisions, and so advanced.

26. This becoming known to the enemy, they suddenly changed their plan, and with their whole force attacked by night the ninth Legion, as being the weakest, and cutting down the sentries, who were asleep or panic-stricken, they broke into the camp. And now the battle was raging within the camp itself, when Agricola, who had learnt from his scouts the enemy's line of march and had kept close on his track, ordered the most active soldiers of his cavalry and infantry to attack the rear of the assailants, while the entire army were shortly to raise a shout. Soon his standards glittered in the light of daybreak. A double peril thus alarmed the Britons, while the courage of the Romans revived; and feeling sure of their safety, they now fought for glory. In their turn they rushed to the attack, and there was a furious conflict within the narrow passages of the gates till the enemy were routed. Both armies did their utmost; the one for the honour of having given aid, the other for that of not having needed support. Had not the flying enemy been sheltered by morasses and forests, this victory would have ended the war.

27. Knowing this, and elated by their glory, our army exclaimed that nothing could resist their valour -- that they must penetrate the recesses of Caledonia, and at length after an unbroken succession

of battles, discover the furthest limits of Britain. Those who but now were cautious and prudent, became after the event eager and boastful. It is the singularly unfair peculiarity of war that the credit of success is claimed by all, while a disaster is attributed to one alone. But the Britons thinking themselves baffled, not so much by our valour as by our general's skilful use of an opportunity, abated nothing of their arrogant demeanour, arming their youth, removing their wives and children to a place of safety, and assembling together to ratify, with sacred rites, a confederacy of all their states. Thus, with angry feelings on both sides, the combatants parted.

28. The same summer a Usipian cohort, which had been levied in Germany and transported into Britain, ventured on a great and memorable exploit. Having killed a centurion and some soldiers, who, to impart military discipline, had been incorporated with their ranks and were employed at once to instruct and command them, they embarked on board three swift galleys with pilots pressed into their service. Under the direction of one of them -- for two of the three they suspected and consequently put to death -- they sailed past the coast in the strangest way before any rumour about them was in circulation. After a while, dispersing in search of water and provisions, they encountered many of the Britons, who sought to defend their property. Often victorious, though now and then beaten, they were at last reduced to such an extremity of want as to be compelled to eat, at first the feeblest of their number, and then victims selected by lot. Having sailed around Britain and lost their vessels from not knowing how to manage them, they were looked upon as pirates and were intercepted, first by the Suevi and then by the Frisii. Some who were sold as slaves in the way of trade and were brought through the process of barter as far as our side of the Rhine, gained notoriety by the disclosure of this extraordinary adventure.

29. Early in the summer Agricola sustained a domestic affliction in the loss of a son born a year before, a calamity which

he endured, neither with the ostentatious fortitude displayed by many brave men, nor, on the other hand, with womanish tears and grief. In his sorrow he found one source of relief in war. Having sent on a fleet, which by its ravages at various points might cause a vague and wide-spread alarm, he advanced with a lightly equipped force, including in its ranks some Britons of remarkable bravery, whose fidelity had been tried through years of peace, as far as the Grampian mountains, which the enemy had already occupied. For the Britons, indeed, in no way cowed by the result of the late engagement, had made up their minds to be either avenged or enslaved, and convinced at length that a common danger must be averted by union, had, by embassies and treaties, summoned forth the whole strength of all their states. More than 30,000 armed men were now to be seen, and still there were pressing in all the youth of the country, with all whose old age was yet hale and vigorous, men renowned in war and bearing each decorations of his own. Meanwhile, among the many leaders, one superior to the rest in valour and in birth, Galgacus by name, is said to have thus harangued the multitude gathered around him and clamouring for battle:-

30. "Whenever I consider the origin of this war and the necessities of our position, I have a sure confidence that this day, and this union of yours, will be the beginning of freedom to the whole of Britain. To all of us slavery is a thing unknown; there are no lands beyond us, and even the sea is not safe, menaced as we are by a Roman fleet. And thus in war and battle, in which the brave find glory, even the coward will find safety. Former contests, in which, with varying fortune, the Romans were resisted, still left in us a last hope of succour, inasmuch as being the most renowned nation of Britain, dwelling in the very heart of the country, and out of sight of the shores of the conquered, we could keep even our eyes unpolluted by the contagion of slavery. To us who dwell on the uttermost confines of the earth and of freedom, this remote sanctuary of Britain's glory has up to this time been a defence.

Now, however, the furthest limits of Britain are thrown open, and the unknown always passes for the marvellous. But there are no tribes beyond us, nothing indeed but waves and rocks, and the yet more terrible Romans, from whose oppression escape is vainly sought by obedience and submission. Robbers of the world, having by their universal plunder exhausted the land, they rifle the deep. If the enemy be rich, they are rapacious; if he be poor, they lust for dominion; neither the east nor the west has been able to satisfy them. Alone among men they covet with equal eagerness poverty and riches. To robbery, slaughter, plunder, they give the lying name of empire; they make a solitude and call it peace.

31. "Nature has willed that every man's children and kindred should be his dearest objects. Yet these are torn from us by conscriptions to be slaves elsewhere. Our wives and our sisters, even though they may escape violation from the enemy, are dishonoured under the names of friendship and hospitality. Our goods and fortunes they collect for their tribute, our harvests for their granaries. Our very hands and bodies, under the lash and in the midst of insult, are worn down by the toil of clearing forests and morasses. Creatures born to slavery are sold once and for all, and are, moreover, fed by their masters; but Britain is daily purchasing, is daily feeding, her own enslaved people. And as in a household the last comer among the slaves is always the butt of his companions, so we in a world long used to slavery, as the newest and most contemptible, are marked out for destruction. We have neither fruitful plains, nor mines, nor harbours, for the working of which we may be spared. Valour, too, and high spirit in subjects, are offensive to rulers; besides, remoteness and seclusion, while they give safety, provoke suspicion. Since then you cannot hope for quarter, take courage, I beseech you, whether it be safety or renown that you hold most precious. Under a woman's leadership the Brigantes were able to burn a colony, to storm a camp, and had not success ended in supineness, might have thrown off the yoke. Let us, then, a fresh and unconquered people, never likely to abuse

our freedom, show forthwith at the very first onset what heroes Caledonia has in reserve.

32. "Do you suppose that the Romans will be as brave in war as they are licentious in peace? To our strifes and discords they owe their fame, and they turn the errors of an enemy to the renown of their own army, an army which, composed as it is of every variety of nations, is held together by success and will be broken up by disaster. These Gauls and Germans, and, I blush to say, these Britons, who, though they lend their lives to support a stranger's rule, have been its enemies longer than its subjects, you cannot imagine to be bound by fidelity and affection. Fear and terror there certainly are, feeble bonds of attachment; remove them, and those who have ceased to fear will begin to hate. All the incentives to victory are on our side. The Romans have no wives to kindle their courage; no parents to taunt them with flight, man have either no country or one far away. Few in number, dismayed by their ignorance, looking around upon a sky, a sea, and forests which are all unfamiliar to them; hemmed in, as it were, and enmeshed, the Gods have delivered them into our hands. Be not frightened by the idle display, by the glitter of gold and of silver, which can neither protect nor wound. In the very ranks of the enemy we shall find our own forces. Britons will acknowledge their own cause; Gauls will remember past freedom; the other Germans will abandon them, as but lately did the Usipii. Behind them there is nothing to dread. The forts are ungarrisoned; the colonies in the hands of aged men; what with disloyal subjects and oppressive rulers, the towns are ill-affected and rife with discord. On the one side you have a general and an army; on the other, tribute, the mines, and all the other penalties of an enslaved people. Whether you endure these for ever, or instantly avenge them, this field is to decide. Think, therefore, as you advance to battle, at once of your ancestors and of your posterity."

33. They received his speech with enthusiasm, and as is usual among barbarians, with songs, shouts, and discordant cries. And

now was seen the assembling of troops and the gleam of arms, as the boldest warriors stepped to the front. As the line was forming, Agricola, who, though his troops were in high spirits and could scarcely be kept within the entrenchments, still thought it right to encourage them, spoke as follows -- "Comrades, this is the eighth year since, thanks to the greatness and good fortune of Rome and to your own loyalty and energy, you conquered Britain. In our many campaigns and battles, whether courage in meeting the foe, or toil and endurance in struggling, I may say, against nature herself, have been needed, I have ever been well satisfied with my soldiers, and you with your commander. And so you and I have passed beyond the limits reached by former armies or by former governors, and we now occupy the last confines of Britain, not merely in rumour and report, but with an actual encampment and armed force. Britain has been both discovered and subdued. Often on the march, when morasses, mountains, and rivers were wearing out your strength, did I hear our bravest men exclaim, 'When shall we have the enemy before us? -- when shall we fight?' He is now here, driven from his lair, and your wishes and your valour have free scope, and everything favours the conqueror, everything is adverse to the vanquished. For as it is a great and glorious achievement, if we press on, to have accomplished so great a march, to have traversed forests and to have crossed estuaries, so, if we retire, our present most complete success will prove our greatest danger. We have not the same knowledge of the country or the same abundance of supplies, but we have arms in our hands, and in them we have everything. For myself I have long been convinced that neither for an army nor for a general is retreat safe. Better, too, is an honourable death than a life of shame, and safety and renown are for us to be found together. And it would be no inglorious end to perish on the extreme confines of earth and of nature.

34. "If unknown nations and an untried enemy confronted you, I should urge you on by the example of other armies. As it is,

look back upon your former honours, question your own eyes. These are the men who last year under cover of darkness attacked a single legion, whom you routed by a shout. Of all the Britons these are the most confirmed runaways, and this is why they have survived so long. Just as when the huntsman penetrates the forest and the thicket, all the most courageous animals rush out upon him, while the timid and feeble are scared away by the very sound of his approach, so the bravest of the Britons have long since fallen; and the rest are a mere crowd of spiritless cowards. You have at last found them, not because they have stood their ground, but because they have been overtaken. Their desperate plight, and the extreme terror that paralyses them, have rivetted their line to this spot, that you might achieve in it a splendid and memorable victory. Put an end to campaigns; crown your fifty years' service with a glorious day; prove to your country that her armies could never have been fairly charged with protracting a war or with causing a rebellion."

35. While Agricola was yet speaking, the ardour of the soldiers was rising to its height, and the close of his speech was followed by a great outburst of enthusiasm. In a moment they flew to arms. He arrayed his eager and impetuous troops in such a manner that the auxiliary infantry, 8,000 in number, strengthened his centre, while 3,000 cavalry were posted on his wings. The legions were drawn up in front of the intrenched camp; his victory would be vastly more glorious if won without the loss of Roman blood, and he would have a reserve in case of repulse. The enemy, to make a more formidable display, had posted himself on high ground; his van was on the plain, while the rest of his army rose in an arch-like form up the slope of a hill. The plain between resounded with the noise and with the rapid movements of chariots and cavalry. Agricola, fearing that from the enemy's superiority of force he would be simultaneously attacked in front and on the flanks, widened his ranks, and though his line was likely to be too extended, and several officers advised him to bring up the legions,

yet, so sanguine was he, so resolute in meeting danger, he sent away his horse and took his stand on foot before the colours.

36. The action began with distant fighting. The Britons with equal steadiness and skill used their huge swords and small shields to avoid or to parry the missiles of our soldiers, while they themselves poured on us a dense shower of darts, till Agricola encouraged three Batavian and two Tungrian cohorts to bring matters to the decision of close fighting with swords. Such tactics were familiar to these veteran soldiers, but were embarrassing to an enemy armed with small bucklers and unwieldy weapons. The swords of the Britons are not pointed, and do not allow them to close with the foe, or to fight in the open field. No sooner did the Batavians begin to close with the enemy, to strike them with their shields, to disfigure their faces, and overthrowing the force on the plain to advance their line up the hill, than the other auxiliary cohorts joined with eager rivalry in cutting down all the nearest of the foe. Many were left behind half dead, some even unwounded, in the hurry of victory. Meantime the enemy's cavalry had fled, and the charioteers had mingled in the engagement of the infantry. But although these at first spread panic, they were soon impeded by the close array of our ranks and by the inequalities of the ground. The battle had anything but the appearance of a cavalry action, for men and horses were carried along in confusion together, while chariots, destitute of guidance, and terrified horses without drivers, dashed as panic urged them, sideways, or in direct collision against the ranks.

37. Those of the Britons who, having as yet taken no part in the engagement, occupied the hill-tops, and who without fear for themselves sat idly disdaining the smallness of our numbers, had begun gradually to descend and to hem in the rear of the victorious army, when Agricola, who feared this very moment, opposed their advance with four squadrons of cavalry held in reserve by him for any sudden emergencies of battle. Their repulse and rout was as severe as their onset had been furious. Thus the enemy's

design recoiled on himself, and the cavalry which by the general's order had wheeled round from the van of the contending armies, attacked his rear. Then, indeed, the open plain presented an awful and hideous spectacle. Our men pursued, wounded, made prisoners of the fugitives only to slaughter them when others fell in their way. And now the enemy, as prompted by their various dispositions, fled in whole battalions with arms in their hands before a few pursuers, while some, who were unarmed, actually rushed to the front and gave themselves up to death. Everywhere there lay scattered arms, corpses, and mangled limbs, and the earth reeked with blood. Even the conquered now and then felt a touch of fury and of courage. On approaching the woods, they rallied, and as they knew the ground, they were able to pounce on the foremost and least cautious of the pursuers. Had not Agricola, who was present everywhere, ordered a force of strong and lightly-equipped cohorts, with some dismounted troopers for the denser parts of the forest, and a detachment of cavalry where it was not so thick, to scour the woods like a party of huntsmen, serious loss would have been sustained through the excessive confidence of our troops. When, however, the enemy saw that we again pursued them in firm and compact array, they fled no longer in masses as before, each looking for his comrade; but dispersing and avoiding one another, they sought the shelter of distant and pathless wilds. Night and weariness of bloodshed put an end to the pursuit. About 10,000 of the enemy were slain; on our side there fell 360 men, and among them Aulus Atticus, the commander of the cohort, whose youthful impetuosity and mettlesome steed had borne him into the midst of the enemy.

38. Elated by their victory and their booty, the conquerors passed a night of merriment. Meanwhile the Britons, wandering amidst the mingled wailings of men and women, were dragging off their wounded, calling to the unhurt, deserting their homes, and in their rage actually firing them, choosing places of concealment only instantly to abandon them. One moment they would take counsel

together, the next, part company, while the sight of those who were dearest to them sometimes melted their hearts, but oftener roused their fury. It was an undoubted fact that some of them vented their rage on their wives and children, as if in pity for their lot. The following day showed more fully the extent of the calamity, for the silence of desolation reigned everywhere: the hills were forsaken, houses were smoking in the distance, and no one was seen by the scouts. These were despatched in all directions; and it having been ascertained that the track of the flying enemy was uncertain, and that there was no attempt at rallying, it being also impossible, as summer was now over, to extend the war, Agricola led back his army into the territory of the Boresti. He received hostages from them, and then ordered the commander of the fleet to sail round Britain. A force for this purpose was given him, which great panic everywhere preceded. Agricola himself, leading his infantry and cavalry by slow marches, so as to overawe the newly-conquered tribes by the very tardiness of his progress, brought them into winter quarters, while the fleet with propitious breezes and great renown entered the harbour of Trutulium, to which it had returned after having coasted along the entire southern shore of the island.

39. Of this series of events, though not exaggerated in the despatches of Agricola by any boastfulness of language, Domitian heard, as was his wont, with joy in his face but anxiety in his heart. He felt conscious that all men laughed at his late mock triumph over Germany, for which there had been purchased from traders people whose dress and hair might be made to resemble those of captives, whereas now a real and splendid victory, with the destruction of thousands of the enemy, was being celebrated with just applause. It was, he thought, a very alarming thing for him that the name of a subject should be raised above that of the Emperor; it was to no purpose that he had driven into obscurity the pursuit of forensic eloquence and the graceful accomplishments of civic life, if another were to forestall the distinctions of war. To other glories he could more easily shut his eyes, but the greatness of a good

general was a truly imperial quality. Harassed by these anxieties, and absorbed in an incommunicable trouble, a sure prognostic of some cruel purpose, he decided that it was best for the present to suspend his hatred until the freshness of Agricola's renown and his popularity with the army should begin to pass away.

40. For Agricola was still the governor of Britain. Accordingly the Emperor ordered that the usual triumphal decorations, the honour of a laurelled statue, and all that is commonly given in place of the triumphal procession, with the addition of many laudatory expressions, should be decreed in the senate, together with a hint to the effect that Agricola was to have the province of Syria, then vacant by the death of Atilius Rufus, a man of consular rank, and generally reserved for men of distinction. It was believed by many persons that one of the freedmen employed on confidential services was sent to Agricola, bearing a despatch in which Syria was offered him, and with instructions to deliver it should he be in Britain; that this freedman in crossing the straights met Agricola, and without even saluting him made his way back to Domitian; though I cannot say whether the story is true, or is only a fiction invented to suit the Emperor's character. Meanwhile Agricola had handed over his province in peace and safety to his successor. And not to make his entrance into Rome conspicuous by the concourse of welcoming throngs, he avoided the attentions of his friends by entering the city at night, and at night too, according to orders, proceded to the palace, where, having been received with a hurried embrace and without a word being spoken, he mingled in the crowd of courtiers. Anxious henceforth to temper the military renown, which annoys men of peace, with other merits, he studiously cultivated retirement and leisure, simple in dress, courteous in conversation, and never accompanied but by one or two friends, so that the many who commonly judge of great men by their external grandeur, after having seen and attentively surveyed him, asked the secret of a greatness which but few could explain.

41. During this time he was frequently accused before Domitian in his absence, and in his absence acquitted. The cause of his danger lay not in any crime, nor in any complaint of injury, but in a ruler who was the foe of virtue, in his own renown, and in that worst class of enemies -- the men who praise. And then followed such days for the commonwealth as would not suffer Agricola to be forgotten; days when so many of our armies were lost in Moesia, Dacia, Germany, and Pannonia, through the rashness or cowardice of our generals, when so many of our officers were besieged and captured with so many of our auxiliaries, when it was no longer the boundaries of empire and the banks of rivers which were imperilled, but the winter-quarters of our legions and the possession of our territories. And so when disaster followed upon disaster, and the entire year was marked by destruction and slaughter, the voice of the people called Agricola to the command; for they all contrasted his vigour, firmness, and experience in war, with the inertness and timidity of other generals. This talk, it is quite certain, assailed the ears of the Emperor himself, while affection and loyalty in the best of his freedmen, malice and envy in the worst, kindled the anger of a prince ever inclined to evil. And so at once, by his own excellences and by the faults of others, Agricola was hurried headlong to a perilous elevation.

42. The year had now arrived in which the pro-consulate of Asia or Africa was to fall to him by lot, and, as Civica had been lately murdered, Agricola did not want a warning, or Domitian a precedent. Persons well acquainted with the Emperor's feelings came to ask Agricola, as if on their own account, whether he would go. First they hinted their purpose by praises of tranquillity and leisure; then offered their services in procuring acceptance for his excuses; and at last, throwing off all disguise, brought him by entreaties and threats to Domitian. The Emperor, armed beforehand with hypocrisy, and assuming a haughty demeanour, listened to his prayer that he might be excused, and having granted his request allowed himself to be formally thanked, nor blushed

to grant so sinister a favour. But the salary usually granted to a pro-consul, and which he had himself given to some governors, he did not bestow on Agricola, either because he was offended at its not having been asked, or was warned by his conscience that he might be thought to have purchased the refusal which he had commanded. It is, indeed, human nature to hate the man whom you have injured; yet the Emperor, notwithstanding his irascible temper and an implacability proportioned to his reserve, was softened by the moderation and prudence of Agricola, who neither by a perverse obstinacy nor an idle parade of freedom challenged fame or provoked his fate. Let it be known to those whose habit it is to admire the disregard of authority, that there may be great men even under bad emperors, and that obedience and submission, when joined to activity and vigour, may attain a glory which most men reach only by a perilous career, utterly useless to the state, and closed by an ostentatious death.

43. The end of his life, a deplorable calamity to us and a grief to his friends, was regarded with concern even by strangers and those who knew him not. The common people and this busy population continually inquired at his house, and talked of him in public places and in private gatherings. No man when he heard of Agricola's death could either be glad or at once forget it. Men's sympathy was increased by a prevalent rumour that he was destroyed by poison. For myself, I have nothing which I should venture to state for fact. Certainly during the whole of his illness the Emperor's chief freedmen and confidential physicians came more frequently than is usual with a court which pays its visits by means of messengers. This was, perhaps, solicitude, perhaps espionage. Certain it is, that on the last day the very agonies of his dying moments were reported by a succession of couriers, and no one believed that there would be such haste about tidings which would be heard with regret. Yet in his manner and countenance the Emperor displayed some signs of sorrow, for he could now forget his enmity, and it was easier to conceal his joy than his fear. It

was well known that on reading the will, in which he was named co-heir with Agricola's excellent wife and most dutiful daughter, he expressed delight, as if it had been a complimentary choice. So blinded and perverted was his mind by incessant flattery, that he did not know that it was only a bad Emperor whom a good father would make his heir.

44. Agricola was born on the 13th of June, in the third consulate of Caius Caesar; he died on the 23rd of August, during the consulate of Collega and Priscus, being in the fifty-sixth year of his age. Should posterity wish to know something of his appearance, it was graceful rather than commanding. There was nothing formidable in his appearance; a gracious look predominated. One would easily believe him a good man, and willingly believe him to be great. As for himself, though taken from us in the prime of a vigorous manhood, yet, as far as glory is concerned, his life was of the longest. Those true blessings, indeed, which consist in virtue, he had fully attained; and on one who had reached the honours of a consulate and a triumph, what more had fortune to bestow? Immense wealth had no attractions for him, and wealth he had, even to splendour. As his daughter and his wife survived him, it may be thought that he was even fortunate -- fortunate, in that while his honours had suffered no eclipse, while his fame was at its height, while his kindred and his friends still prospered, he escaped from the evil to come. For, though to survive until the dawn of this most happy age and to see a Trajan on the throne was what he would speculate upon in previsions and wishes confided to my ears, yet he had this mighty compensation for his premature death, that he was spared those later years during which Domitian, leaving now no interval or breathing space of time, but, as it were, with one continuous blow, drained the life-blood of the Commonwealth.

45. Agricola did not see the senate-house besieged, or the senate hemmed in by armed men, or so many of Rome's noblest ladies exiles and fugitives. Carus Metius had as yet the distinction of but

one victory, and the noisy counsels of Messalinus were not heard beyond the walls of Alba, and Massa Baebius was then answering for his life. It was not long before our hands dragged Helvidius to prison, before we gazed on the dying looks of Manricus and Rusticus, before we were steeped in Senecio's innocent blood. Even Nero turned his eyes away, and did not gaze upon the atrocities which he ordered; with Domitian it was the chief part of our miseries to see and to be seen, to know that our sighs were being recorded, to have, ever ready to note the pallid looks of so many faces, that savage countenance reddened with the hue with which he defied shame.

Thou wast indeed fortunate, Agricola, not only in the splendour of thy life, but in the opportune moment of thy death. Thou submittedst to thy fate, so they tell us who were present to hear thy last words, with courage and cheerfulness, seeming to be doing all thou couldst to give thine Emperor full acquittal. As for me and thy daughter, besides all the bitterness of a father's loss, it increases our sorrow that it was not permitted us to watch over thy failing health, to comfort thy weakness, to satisfy ourselves with those looks, those embraces. Assuredly we should have received some precepts, some utterances to fix in our inmost hearts. This is the bitterness of our sorrow, this the smart of our wound, that from the circumstance of so long an absence thou wast lost to us four years before. Doubtless, best of fathers, with that most loving wife at thy side, all the dues of affection were abundantly paid thee, yet with too few tears thou wast laid to thy rest, and in the light of thy last day there was something for which thine eyes longed in vain.

46. If there is any dwelling-place for the spirits of the just; if, as the wise believe, noble souls do not perish with the body, rest thou in peace; and call us, thy family, from weak regrets and womanish laments to the contemplation of thy virtues, for which we must not weep nor beat the breast. Let us honour thee not so much with transitory praises as with our reverence, and, if our powers permit us, with our emulation. That will be true respect,

that the true affection of thy nearest kin. This, too, is what I would enjoin on daughter and wife, to honour the memory of that father, that husband, by pondering in their hearts all his words and acts, by cherishing the features and lineaments of his character rather than those of his person. It is not that I would forbid the likenesses which are wrought in marble or in bronze; but as the faces of men, so all similitudes of the face are weak and perishable things, while the fashion of the soul is everlasting, such as may be expressed not in some foreign substance, or by the help of art, but in our own lives. Whatever we loved, whatever we admired in Agricola, survives, and will survive in the hearts of men, in the succession of the ages, in the fame that waits on noble deeds. Over many indeed, of those who have gone before, as over the inglorious and ignoble, the waves of oblivion will roll; Agricola, made known to posterity by history and tradition, will live for ever.

A TREATISE ON THE SITUATION, MANNERS AND INHABITANTS OF GERMANY

1. Germany[1] is separated from Gaul, Rhaetia[2], and Pannonia[3], [4] by the rivers Rhine and Danube; from Sarmatia and Dacia, by mountains[4] and mutual dread. The rest is surrounded by an ocean, embracing broad promontories[5] and vast insular tracts[6], in which our military expeditions have lately discovered various nations and kingdoms. The Rhine, issuing from the inaccessible and precipitous summit of the Rhaetic Alps[7], bends gently to the west, and falls into the Northern Ocean. The Danube, poured from the easy and gently raised ridge of Mount Abnoba[8], visits several

---

1 The Germany here meant is that beyond the Rhine. The Germania Cisrhenana, divided into the Upper and Lower, was a part of Gallia Belgica.

2 Rhaetia comprehended the country of the Grisons, with part of Suabia and Bavaria.

3 Lower Hungary, and part of Austria.

4 The Carpathian mountains in Upper Hungary.

5 "Broad promontories." Latos sinus. Sinus strictly signifies "a bending," especially inwards. Hence it is applied to a gulf, or bay, of the sea. And hence, again, by metonymy, to that projecting part of the land, whereby the gulf is formed; and still further to any promontory or peninsula. It is in this latter force it is here used; - and refers especially to the Danish peninsula. See Livy xxvii, 30, xxxviii. 5; Servius on Virgil, Aen. xi. 626.

6 Scandinavia and Finland, of which the Romans had a very slight knowledge, were supposed to be islands.

7 The mountains of the Grisons. That in which the Rhine rises is at present called Vogelberg.

8 Now called Schwartzwald, or the Black Forest. The name Danubius was given to that portion of the river which is included between its source and Vindobona (Vienna); throughout the rest of its course it was called Ister.

nations in its course, till at length it bursts out[9] by six channels[10] into the Pontic sea; a seventh is lost in marshes.

2. The people of Germany appear to me indigenous[11], and free from intermixture with foreigners, either as settlers or casual visitants. For the emigrants of former ages performed their expeditions not by land, but by water[12]; and that immense, and, if I may so call it, hostile ocean, is rarely navigated by ships from our world.[13] Then, besides the danger of a boisterous and unknown sea, who would relinquish Asia, Africa, or Italy, for Germany, a land rude in its surface, rigorous in its climate, cheerless to every beholder and cultivator, except a native? In their ancient songs[14], which are their only records or annals, they celebrate the god Tuisto[15], sprung from the earth, and his son Mannus, as

---

9 Donec erumpat. The term erumpat is most correctly and graphically employed; for the Danube discharges its waters into the Euxine with so great force, that its course may be distinctly traced for miles out to sea.

10 There are now but five.

11 The ancient writers called all nations indigenae (i.e. inde geniti), or autochthones, "sprung from the soil," of whose origin they were ignorant.

12 It is, however, well established that the ancestors of the Germans migrated by land from Asia. Tacitus here falls into a very common kind of error, in assuming a local fact (viz. the manner in which migrations took place in the basin of the Mediterranean) to be the expression of a general law. - ED.

13 Drusus, father of the emperor Claudius, was the first Roman general who navigated the German Ocean. The difficulties and dangers which Germanicus met with from the storms of this sea are related in the Annals, ii. 23.

14 All barbarous nations, in all ages, have applied verse to the same use, as is still found to be the case among the North American Indians. Charlemagne, as we are told by Eginhart, "wrote out and committed to memory barbarous verses of great antiquity, in which the actions and wars of ancient kings were recorded."

15 The learned Leibnitz supposes this Tuisto to have been the Teut or Teutates so famous throughout Gaul and Spain, who was a Celto-Scythian king or hero, and subdued and civilized a great part of Europe and Asia. Various other conjectures have been formed concerning him and his son Mannus, but most of

the fathers and founders of their race. To Mannus they ascribe three sons, from whose names[16] the people bordering on the ocean are called Ingaevones; those inhabiting the central parts, Herminones; the rest, Istaevones. Some[17], however, assuming the licence of antiquity, affirm that there were more descendants of the god, from whom more appellations were derived; as those of the Marsi[18], Gambrivii[19], Suevi[20], and Vandali[21]; and that these are

---

them extremely vague and improbable. Among the rest, it has been thought that in Mannus and his three sons an obscure tradition is preserved of Adam, and his sons Cain, Abel, and Seth; or of Noah, and his sons Shem, Ham, and Japhet.

16 Conringius interprets the names of the sons of Mannus into Ingäff, Istäf, and Hermin.

17 Pliny, iv. 14, embraces a middle opinion between these, and mentions five capital tribes. The Vindili, to whom belong the Burgundiones, Varini, Carini, and Guttones; the Ingaevones, including the Cimbri, Teutoni, and Chauci; the Istaevones, near the Rhine, part of whom are the midland Cimbri; the Hermiones, containing the Suevi, Hermunduri, Catti, and Cherusci; and the Peucini and Bastarnae, bordering upon the Dacians.

18 The Marsi appear to have occupied various portions of the northwest part of Germany at various times. In the time of Tiberius (A.D. 14) they sustained a great slaughter from the forces of Germanicus, who ravaged their country for fifty miles with fire and sword, sparing neither age nor sex, neither things profane nor sacred. (See Ann. i. 51.) At this period they were occupying the country in the neighborhood of the Rura (Ruhr), a tributary of the Rhine. Probably this slaughter was the destruction of them as a separate people; and by the time that Trajan succeeded to the imperial power they seem to have been blotted out from amongst the Germanic tribes. Hence their name will not be found in the following account of Germany.

19 These people are mentioned by Strabo, vii. 1, 3. Their locality is not very easy to determine.

20 See note, c. 38.

21 The Vandals are said to have derived their name from the German word wendeln, "to wander." They began to be troublesome to the Romans A.D. 160, in the reigns of Aurelius and Verus. In A.D. 410 they made themselves masters of Spain in conjunction with the Alans and Suevi, and received for their share what from them was termed Vandalusia (Andalusia). In A.D. 429 they crossed

the genuine and original names[22]. That of Germany, on the other hand, they assert to be a modern addition[23]; for that the people who first crossed the Rhine, and expelled the Gauls, and are now called Tungri, were then named Germans; which appellation of a particular tribe, not of a whole people, gradually prevailed; so that the title of Germans, first assumed by the victors in order to excite terror, was afterwards adopted by the nation in general[24]. They have likewise the tradition of a Hercules[25] of their country, whose praises they sing before those of all other heroes as they advance to battle.

---

into Africa under Genseric, who not only made himself master of Byzacium, Gaetulia, and part of Numidia, but also crossed over into Italy, A.D. 455, and plundered Rome. After the death of Genseric the Vandal power declined.

22 That is, those of the Marsi, Gambrivii, etc. Those of Ingaevones, Istaevones, and Hermiones, were not so much names of the people, as terms expressing their situation. For, according to the most learned Germans, the Ingaevones are die Inwohner, those dwelling inwards, towards the sea; the Istaevones, die Westwohner, the inhabitants of the western parts: and the Hermiones, die Herumwohner, the midland inhabitants.

23 It is however found in an inscription so far back as the year of Rome 531, before Christ 222, recording the victory of Claudius Marcellus over the Galli Insubres and their allies the Germans, at Clastidium, now Chiastezzo in the Milanese.

24 This is illustrated by a passage in Caesar, Bell. Gall. ii. 4, where, after mentioning that several of the Belgae were descended from the Germans who had formerly crossed the Rhine and expelled the Gauls, he says, "the first of these emigrants were the Condrusii, Eburones, Caeresi and Paemani, who were called by the common name of Germans." The derivation of German is Wehr mann, a warrior, or man of war. This appellation was first used by the victorious Cisrhenane tribes, but not by the whole Transrhenane nation, till they gradually adopted it, as equally due to them on account of their military reputation. The Tungri were formerly a people of great name, the relics of which still exist in the extent of the district now termed the ancient diocese of Tongres.

25 Under this name Tacitus speaks of some German deity, whose attributes corresponded in the main with those of the Greek and Roman Hercules. What he was called by the Germans is a matter of doubt. - White.

3. A peculiar kind of verses is also current among them, by the recital of which, termed "barding,"[26] they stimulate their courage; while the sound itself serves as an augury of the event of the impending combat. For, according to the nature of the cry proceeding from the line, terror is inspired or felt: nor does it seem so much an articulate song, as the wild chorus of valor. A harsh, piercing note, and a broken roar, are the favorite tones; which they render more full and sonorous by applying their mouths to their shields[27]. Some conjecture that Ulysses, in the course of his long

---

26 Quem barditum vocant. The word barditus is of Gallic origin, being derived from bardi, "bards;" it being a custom with the Gauls for bards to accompany the army, and celebrate the heroic deeds of their great warriors; so that barditum would thus signify "the fulfilment of the bard's office." Hence it is clear that barditum could not be used correctly here, inasmuch as amongst the Germans not any particular, appointed, body of men, but the whole army chanted forth the war-song. Some editions have baritum, which is said to be derived from the German word beren, or baeren, "to shout;" and hence it is translated in some dictionaries as, "the German war-song." From the following passage extracted from Facciolati, it would seem, however, that German critics repudiate this idea: "De barito clamore bellico, seu, ut quaedam habent exemplaria, bardito, nihil audiuimus nunc in Germaniâ: nisi hoc dixerimus, quòd bracht, vel brecht, milites Germani appellare consueverunt; concursum videlicet certantium, et clamorem ad pugnam descendentium; quem bar, bar, bar, sonuisse nonnulli affirmant." - (Andr. Althameri, Schol. in C. Tacit De Germanis.) Ritter, himself a German, affirms that baritus is a reading worth nothing; and that barritus was not the name of the ancient German war-song, but of the shout raised by the Romans in later ages when on the point of engaging; and that it was derived "a clamore barrorem, i.e. elephantorum." The same learned editor considers that the words "quem barditum vocant" have been originally the marginal annotation of some unsound scholar, and have been incorporated by some transcriber into the text of his MS. copy, whence the error has spread. He therefore encloses them between brackets, to show that, in his judgment, they are not the genuine production of the pen of Tacitus. - White.

27 A very curious coincidence with the ancient German opinion concerning the prophetic nature of the war-cry or song, appears in the following passage of the Life of Sir Ewen Cameron, in "Pennant's Tour," 1769, Append, p. 363. At the battle of Killicrankie, just before the fight began, "he (Sir Ewen) commanded such of the Camerons as were posted near him to make a great

and fabulous wanderings, was driven into this ocean, and landed in Germany; and that Asciburgium[28], a place situated on the Rhine, and at this day inhabited, was founded by him, and named Askipurgion. They pretend that an altar was formerly discovered here, consecrated to Ulysses, with the name of his father Laertes subjoined; and that certain monuments and tombs, inscribed with Greek characters[29], are still extant upon the confines of Germany and Rhaetia. These allegations I shall neither attempt to confirm nor to refute: let every one believe concerning them as he is disposed.

4. I concur in opinion with those who deem the Germans never to have intermarried with other nations; but to be a race, pure, unmixed, and stamped with a distinct character. Hence a family likeness pervades the whole, though their numbers are so great: eyes stern and blue; ruddy hair; large bodies[30], powerful in sudden

---

shout, which being seconded by those who stood on the right and left, ran quickly through the whole army, and was returned by the enemy. But the noise of the muskets and cannon, with the echoing of the hills, made the Highlanders fancy that their shouts were much louder and brisker than those of the enemy, and Lochiel cried out, 'Gentlemen, take courage, the day is ours: I am the oldest commander in the army, and have always observed something ominous and fatal in such a dull, hollow and feeble noise as the enemy made in their shout, which prognosticates that they are all doomed to die by our hands this night; whereas ours was brisk, lively and strong, and shows we have vigor and courage.' These words, spreading quickly through the army, animated the troops in a strange manner. The event justified the prediction; the Highlanders obtained a complete victory."

28 Now Asburg in the county of Meurs.

29 The Greeks, by means of their colony at Marseilles, introduced their letters into Gaul, and the old Gallic coins have many Greek characters in their inscriptions. The Helvetians also, as we are informed by Caesar, used Greek letters. Thence they might easily pass by means of commercial intercourse to the neighboring Germans. Count Marsili and others have found monuments with Greek inscriptions in Germany, but not of so early an age.

30 The large bodies of the Germans are elsewhere taken notice of by Tacitus,

exertions, but impatient of toil and labor, least of all capable of sustaining thirst and heat. Cold and hunger they are accustomed by their climate and soil to endure.

5. The land, though varied to a considerable extent in its aspect, is yet universally shagged with forests, or deformed by marshes: moister on the side of Gaul, more bleak on the side of Norieum and Pannonia[31]. It is productive of grain, but unkindly to fruit-trees[32]. It abounds in flocks and herds, but in general of a small breed. Even the beeve kind are destitute of their usual stateliness and dignity of head[33]: they are, however, numerous, and form the most esteemed, and, indeed, the only species of wealth. Silver and gold the gods, I know not whether in their favor or anger, have denied to this country[34]. Not that I would assert that no veins of these metals are generated in Germany; for who has made the search? The possession of them is not coveted by these people as it is by us. Vessels of silver are indeed to be seen among them, which have been presented to their ambassadors and chiefs; but they are held in no higher estimation than earthenware. The borderers, however, set a value on gold and silver for the purpose of commerce, and have learned to distinguish several kinds of our coin, some of which

---

and also by other authors. It would appear as if most of them were at that time at least six feet high. They are still accounted some of the tallest people in Europe.

31 Bavaria and Austria.

32 The greater degree of cold when the country was overspread with woods and marshes, made this observation more applicable than at present. The same change of temperature from clearing and draining the land has taken place in North America. It may be added, that the Germans, as we are afterwards informed, paid attention to no kind of culture but that of corn.

33 The cattle of some parts of Germany are at present remarkably large; so that their former smallness must have rather been owing to want of care in feeding them and protecting them from the inclemencies of winter, and in improving the breed by mixtures, than to the nature of the climate.

34 Mines both of gold and silver have since been discovered in Germany; the former, indeed, inconsiderable; but the latter, valuable.

they prefer to others: the remoter inhabitants continue the more simple and ancient usage of bartering commodities. The money preferred by the Germans is the old and well-known species, such as the Serrati and Bigati[35]. They are also better pleased with silver than gold[36]; not on account of any fondness for that metal, but because the smaller money is more convenient in their common and petty merchandise.

6. Even iron is not plentiful[37] among them; as may be inferred from the nature of their weapons. Swords or broad lances are seldom used; but they generally carry a spear, (called in their language framea[38]), which has an iron blade, short and narrow, but so sharp and manageable, that, as occasion requires, they

---

35 As vice and corruption advanced among the Romans, their money became debased and adulterated. Thus Pliny, xxxiii. 3, relates, that "Livius Drusus during his tribuneship, mixed an eighth part of brass with the silver coin;" and ibid. 9, "that Antony the triumvir mixed iron with the denarius: that some coined base metal, others diminished the pieces, and hence it became an art to prove the goodness of the denarii." One precaution for this purpose was cutting the edges like the teeth of a saw, by which means it was seen whether the metal was the same quite through, or was only plated. These were the Serrati, or serrated Denarii. The Bigati were those stamped with the figure of a chariot drawn by two horses, as were the Quadrigati with a chariot and four horses. These were old coin, of purer silver than those of the emperors. Hence the preference of the Germans for certain kinds of species was founded on their apprehension of being cheated with false money.

36 The Romans had the same predilection for silver coin, and probably on the same account originally. Pliny, in the place above cited, expresses his surprise that "the Roman people had always imposed a tribute in silver on conquered nations; as at the end of the second Punic war, when they demanded an annual payment in silver for fifty years, without any gold."

37 Iron was in great abundance in the bowels of the earth; but this barbarous people had neither patience, skill, nor industry to dig and work it. Besides, they made use of weapons of stone, great numbers of which are found in ancient tombs and barrows.

38 This is supposed to take its name from pfriem or priem, the point of a weapon. Afterwards, when iron grew more plentiful, the Germans chiefly used swords.

employ it either in close or distant fighting[39]. This spear and a shield are all the armor of the cavalry. The foot have, besides, missile weapons, several to each man, which they hurl to an immense distance[40]. They are either naked[41], or lightly covered with a small mantle; and have no pride in equipage: their shields only are ornamented with the choicest colors.[42] Few are provided with a coat of mail[43]; and scarcely here and there one with a casque or helmet[44]. Their horses are neither remarkable for beauty nor swiftness, nor are they taught the various evolutions practised with us. The cavalry either bear down straight forwards, or wheel

39 It appears, however, from Tacitus's Annals, ii. 14, that the length of these spears rendered them unmanageable in an engagement among trees and bushes.

40 Notwithstanding the manner of fighting is so much changed in modern times, the arms of the ancients are still in use. We, as well as they, have two kinds of swords, the sharp-pointed, and edged (small sword and sabre). The broad lance subsisted till lately in the halberd; the spear and framea in the long pike and spontoon; the missile weapons in the war hatchet, or North American tomahawk. There are, besides, found in the old German barrows, perforated stone balls, which they threw by means of thongs passed through them.

41 Nudi. The Latin nudus, like the Greek gemnos, does not point out a person devoid of all clothing, but merely one without an upper garment - clad merely in a vest or tunic, and that perhaps a short one. - White.

42 This decoration at first denoted the valor, afterwards the nobility, of the bearer; and in process of time gave origin to the armorial ensigns so famous in the ages of chivalry. The shields of the private men were simply colored; those of the chieftains had the figures of animals painted on them.

43 Plutarch, in his Life of Marius, describes somewhat differently the arms and equipage of the Cimbri. "They wore (says he) helmets representing the heads of wild beasts, and other unusual figures, and crowned with a winged crest, to make them appear taller. They were covered with iron coats of mail, and carried white glittering shields. Each had a battle- axe; and in close fight they used large heavy swords." But the learned Eccard justly observes, that they had procured these arms in their march; for the Holsatian barrows of that age contain few weapons of brass, and none of iron; but stone spear-heads, and instead of swords, the wedgelike bodies vulgarly called thunderbolts.

44 Casques (cassis) are of metal; helmets (galea) of leather - Isidorus.

once to the right, in so compact a body that none is left behind the rest. Their principal strength, on the whole, consists in their infantry: hence in an engagement these are intermixed with the cavalry[45]; so Well accordant with the nature of equestrian combats is the agility of those foot soldiers, whom they select from the whole body of their youth, and place in the front of the line. Their number, too, is determined; a hundred from each canton[46]: and they are distinguished at home by a name expressive of this circumstance; so that what at first was only an appellation of number, becomes thenceforth a title of honor. Their line of battle is disposed in wedges[47]. To give ground, provided they rally again,

---

45 This mode of fighting is admirably described by Caesar. "The Germans engaged after the following manner: - There were 6,000 horse, and an equal number of the swiftest and bravest foot; who were chosen, man by man, by the cavalry, for their protection. By these they were attended in battle; to these they retreated; and, these, if they were hard pressed, joined them in the combat. If any fell wounded from their horses, by these they were covered. If it were necessary to advance or retreat to any considerable distance, such agility had they acquired by exercise, that, supporting themselves by the horses' manes, they kept pace with them." - Bell. Gall. i. 48.

46 To understand this, it is to be remarked, that the Germans were divided into nations or tribes, - these into cantons, and these into districts or townships. The cantons (pagi in Latin) were called by themselves gauen. The districts or townships (vici) were called hunderte, whence the English hundreds. The name given to these select youth, according to the learned Dithmar, was die hunderte, hundred men. From the following passage in Caesar, it appears that in the more powerful tribes a greater number was selected from each canton. "The nation of the Suevi is by far the greatest and most warlike of the Germans. They are said to inhabit a hundred cantons; from each of which a thousand men are sent annually to make war out of their own territories. Thus neither the employments of agriculture, nor the use of arms are interrupted." - Bell. Gall. iv. 1. The warriors were summoned by the heribannum, or army- edict; whence is derived the French arrière-ban.

47 A wedge is described by Vegetius (iii. 19,) as a body of infantry, narrow in front, and widening towards the rear; by which disposition they were enabled to break the enemy's ranks, as all their weapons were directed to one spot. The soldiers called it a boar's head.

is considered rather as a prudent strategem, than cowardice. They carry off their slain even while the battle remains undecided. The, greatest disgrace that can befall them is to have abandoned their shields[48]. A person branded with this ignominy is not permitted to join in their religious rites, or enter their assemblies; so that many, after escaping from battle, have put an end to their infamy by the halter.

7. In the election of kings they have regard to birth; in that of generals[49], to valor. Their kings have not an absolute or unlimited power[50]; and their generals command less through the force of authority, than of example. If they are daring, adventurous, and conspicuous in action, they procure obedience from the admiration they inspire. None, however, but the priests[51] are permitted to judge offenders, to inflict bonds or stripes; so that chastisement

---

48 It was also considered as the height of injury to charge a person with this unjustly. Thus, by the Salic law, tit. xxxiii, 5, a fine of 600 denarii (about 9_l._) is imposed upon "every free man who shall accuse another of throwing down his shield, and running away, without being able to prove it."

49 Vertot (Mém. de l'Acad. des Inscrip.) supposes that the French maires du palais had their origin from these German military leaders. If the kings were equally conspicuous for valor as for birth, they united the regal with the military command. Usually, however, several kings and generals were assembled in their wars. In this case, the most eminent commanded, and obtained a common jurisdiction in war, which did not subsist in time of peace. Thus Caesar (Bell. Gall. vi.) says, "In peace they have no common magistracy." A general was elected by placing him on a shield, and lifting him on the shoulders of the bystanders. The same ceremonial was observed in the election of kings.

50 Hence Ambiorix, king of the Eburones, declare that "the nature of his authority was such, that the people had no less power over him, than he over the people." - Caesar, Bell. Gall. v. The authority of the North American chiefs almost exactly similar.

51 The power of life and death, however, was in the hands of magistrates. Thus Caesar: "When a state engages either in an offensive or defensive war, magistrates are chosen to preside over it, and exercise power of life and death." - Bell. Gall. vi. The infliction of punishments was committed to the priests, in order to give them more solemnity, and render them less invidious.

appears not as an act of military discipline, but as the instigation of the god whom they suppose present with warriors. They also carry with them to battle certain images and standards taken from the sacred groves[52]. It is a principal incentive to their courage, that their squadrons and battalions are not formed by men fortuitously collected, but by the assemblage of families and clans. Their pledges also are near at hand; they have within hearing the yells of their women, and the cries of their children. These, too, are the most revered witnesses of each man's conduct, these his most liberal applauders. To their mothers and their wives they bring their wounds for relief, nor do these dread to count or to search out the gashes. The women also administer food and encouragement to those who are fighting.

8. Tradition relates, that armies beginning to give way have been rallied by the females, through the earnestness of their supplications, the interposition of their bodies[53], and the pictures they have drawn of impending slavery[54], a calamity which these

---

52 Effigiesque et signa quaedam. That effigies does not mean the images of their deities is proved by that is stated at chap. ix., viz. that they deemed it derogatory to their deities to represent them in human form; and, if in human form, we may argue, a fortiori, in the form of the lower animals. The interpretation of the passage will be best derived from Hist. iv. 22, where Tacitus says: - "Depromptae silvis lucisve ferarum imagines, ut cuique genti inire praelium mos est." It would hence appear that these effigies and signa were images of wild animals, and were national standards preserved with religious care in sacred woods and groves, whence they were brought forth when the clan or tribe was about to take the field. - White.

53 They not only interposed to prevent the flight of their husbands and sons, but, in desperate emergencies, themselves engaged in battle. This happened on Marius's defeat of the Cimbri (hereafter to be mentioned); and Dio relates, that when Marcus Aurelius overthrew the Marcomanni, Quadi, and other German allies, the bodies of women in armor were found among the slain.

54 Thus, in the army of Ariovistus, the women, with their hair dishevelled, and weeping, besought the soldiers not to deliver them captives to the Romans. - Caesar, Bell. Gall. i.

people bear with more impatience for their women than themselves; so that those states who have been obliged to give among their hostages the daughters of noble families, are the most effectually bound to fidelity[55]. They even suppose somewhat of sanctity and prescience to be inherent in the female sex; and therefore neither despise their counsels[56], nor disregard their responses[57]. We have beheld, in the reign of Vespasian, Veleda[58], long reverenced by many as a deity. Aurima, moreover, and several others[59], were

---

55 Relative to this, perhaps, is a circumstance mentioned by Suetonius in his Life of Augustus. "From some nations he attempted to exact a new kind of hostages, women: because he observed that those of the male sex were disregarded." - Aug. xxi.

56 See the same observation with regard to the Celtic women, in Plutarch, on the virtues of women. The North Americans pay a similar regard to their females.

57 A remarkable instance of this is given by Caesar. "When he inquired of the captives the reason why Ariovistus did not engage, he learned, that it was because the matrons, who among the Germans are accustomed to pronounce, from their divinations, whether or not a battle will be favorable, had declared that they would not prove victorious, if they should fight before the new moon." - Bell. Gall. i. The cruel manner in which the Cimbrian women performed their divinations is thus related by Strabo: "The women who follow the Cimbri to war, are accompanied by gray- haired prophetesses, in white vestments, with canvas mantles fastened by clasps, a brazen girdle, and naked feet. These go with drawn swords through the camp, and, striking down those of the prisoners that they meet, drag them to a brazen kettle, holding about twenty amphorae. This has a kind of stage above it, ascending on which, the priestess cuts the throat of the victim, and, from the manner in which the blood flows into the vessel, judges of the future event. Others tear open the bodies of the captives thus butchered, and, from inspection of the entrails, presage victory to their own party." - Lib. vii.

58 She was afterwards taken prisoner by Rutilius Gallicus. Statius, in his Sylvae, i. 4, refers to this event. Tacitus has more concerning her in his History, iv. 61.

59 Viradesthis was a goddess of the Tungri; Harimella, another provincial deity; whose names were found by Mr. Pennant inscribed on altars at the Roman station at Burrens. These were erected by the German auxiliaries. - Vide Tour in Scotland, 1772, part ii. p. 406.

formerly held in equal veneration, but not with a servile flattery, nor as though they made them goddesses.[60]

9. Of the gods, Mercury[61] is the principal object of their adoration; whom, on certain days[62], they think it lawful to

---

60 Ritter considers that here is a reference to the servile flattery of the senate as exhibited in the time of Nero, by the deification of Poppaea's infant daughter, and afterwards of herself. (See Ann. xv. 23, Dion. lxiii, Ann. xiv. 3.) There is no contradiction in the present passage to that found at Hist. iv. 61, where Tacitus says, "plerasque feminarum fatidicas et, augescente superstitione, arbitrantur deas;" i.e. they deem (arbitrantur) very many of their women possessed of prophetic powers, and, as their religious feeling increases, they deem (arbitrantur) them goddesses, i.e. possessed of a superhuman nature; they do not, however, make them goddesses and worship them, as the Romans did Poppaea and her infant, which is covertly implied in facerent deas. - White.

61 Mercury, i.e. a god whom Tacitus thus names, because his attributes resembled those of the Roman Mercury. According to Paulus Diaconus (de Gestis Langobardorum, i. 9), this deity was Wodun, or Gwodan, called also Odin. Mallet (North. Ant. ch. v.) says, that in the Icelandic mythology he is called "the terrible and severe God, the Father of Slaughter, he who giveth victory and receiveth courage in the conflict, who nameth those that are to be slain." "The Germans drew their gods by their own character, who loved nothing so much themselves as to display their strength and power in battle, and to signalize their vengeance upon their enemies by slaughter and desolation." There remain to this day some traces of the worship paid to Odin in the name given by almost all the people of the north to the fourth day of the week, which was formerly consecrated to him. It is called by a name which signifies "Odin's day;" "Old Norse, Odinsdagr; Swedish and Danish, Onsdag; Anglo-Saxon, Wodenesdaeg, Wodnesdaeg; Dutch, Woensdag; English, Wednesday. As Odin or Wodun was supposed to correspond to the Mercury of the Greeks and Romans, the name of this day was expressed in Latin Dies Mercurii." - White.

62 "The appointed time for these sacrifices," says Mallet (North. Ant. ch. vi.), "was always determined by a superstitious opinion which made the northern nations regard the number 'three' as sacred and particularly dear to the gods. Thus, in every ninth month they renewed the bloody ceremony, which was to last nine days, and every day they offered up nine living victims, whether men or animals. But the most solemn sacrifices were those which were offered up at Upsal in Sweden every ninth year...." After stating the compulsory nature of the attendance at this festival, Mallet adds, "Then they chose among the

propitiate even with human victims. To Hercules and Mars[63] they offer the animals usually allotted for sacrifice[64]. Some of the Suevi also perform sacred rites to Isis. What was the cause and origin of this foreign worship, I have not been able to discover; further than that her being represented with the symbol of a galley, seems to indicate an imported religion[65]. They conceive it unworthy the

---

captives in time of war, and among the slaves in time of peace, nine persons to be sacrificed. In whatever manner they immolated men, the priest always took care in consecrating the victim to pronounce certain words, as 'I devote thee to Odin,' 'I send thee to Odin.'" See Lucan i. 444.

"Et quibus immitis placatur sanguine diro

Teutates, horrensque feris altaribus Hesus."

Teutates is Mercury, Hesus, Mars. So also at iii. 399, &c.

"Lucus erat longo nunquam violatus ab aevo.

… Barbara ritu

Sacra Deum, structae diris altaribus arae,

Omnis et humanis lustrata cruoribus arbor."

63 That is, as in the preceding case, a deity whose attributes corresponded to those of the Roman Mars. This appears to have been not Thor, who is rather the representative of the Roman Jupiter, but Tyr, "a warrior god, and the protector of champions and brave men!" "From Tyr is derived the name given to the third day of the week in most of the Teutonic languages, and which has been rendered into Latin by Dies Martis. Old Norse, Tirsdagr, Tisdagr; Swedish, Tisdag; Danish, Tirsdag; German, Dienstag; Dutch, Dingsdag; Anglo-Saxon, Tyrsdaeg, Tyvesdag, Tivesdaeg; English, Tuesday" - (Mallet's North. Ant. ch. v.) - White.

64 The Suevi appear to have been the Germanic tribes, and this also the worship spoken of at chap. xl. _Signum in modum liburnae figuration _corresponds with the vehiculum there spoken of; the real thing being, according to Ritter's view, a pinnace placed on wheels. That signum ipsum ("the very symbol") does not mean any image of the goddess, may be gathered also from ch. xl., where the goddess herself, si credere velis, is spoken of as being washed in the sacred lake.

65 As the Romans in their ancient coins, many of which are now extant, recorded the arrival of Saturn by the stern of a ship; so other nations have frequently denoted the importation of a foreign religious rite by the figure of a galley on their medals.

grandeur of celestial beings to confine their deities within walls, or to represent them under a human similitude[66]: woods and groves are their temples; and they affix names of divinity to that secret power, which they behold with the eye of adoration alone.

10. No people are more addicted to divination by omens and lots. The latter is performed in the following simple manner. They cut a twig[67] from a fruit-tree, and divide it into small pieces, which, distinguished by certain marks, are thrown promiscuously upon a white garment. Then, the priest of the canton, if the occasion be public; if private, the master of the family; after an invocation of the gods, with his eyes lifted up to heaven, thrice takes out each piece, and, as they come up, interprets their signification according to the marks fixed upon them. If the result prove unfavorable, there is no more consultation on the same affair that day; if propitious, a confirmation by omens is still required. In common with other nations, the Germans are acquainted with the practice of auguring from the notes and flight of birds; but it is peculiar to them to derive admonitions and presages from horses also[68].

---

66 Tacitus elsewhere speaks of temples of German divinities (e.g. 40; Templum Nerthae, Ann. i. 51; Templum Tanfanae); but a consecrated grove, or any other sacred place, was called templum by the Romans.

67 The Scythians are mentioned by Herodotus, and the Alans by Ammianus Marcellinus, as making use of these divining rods. The German method of divination with them is illustrated by what is said by Saxo-Grammaticus (Hist. Dan. xiv, 288) of the inhabitants of the Isle of Rugen in the Baltic Sea: "Throwing, by way of lots, three pieces of wood, white in one part, and black in another, into their laps, they foretold good fortune by the coming up of the white; bad by that of the black."

68 Same practice obtained among the Persians, from whom the Germans appear to be sprung. Darius was elected king by the neighing of a horse; sacred white horses were in the army of Cyrus; and Xerxes, retreating after his defeat, was preceded by the sacred horses and consecrated chariot. Justin (i. 10) mentions the cause of this superstition, viz. that "the Persians believed the Sun to be the only God, and horses to be peculiarly consecrated to him." Priest of the Isle of Rugen also took auspices from a white horse, as may be seen in Saxo-Grammaticus.

Certain of these animals, milk-white, and untouched by earthly labor, are pastured at the public expense in the sacred woods and groves. These, yoked to a consecrated chariot, are accompanied by the priest, and king, or chief person of the community, who attentively observe their manner of neighing and snorting; and no kind of augury is more credited, not only among the populace, but among the nobles and priests. For the latter consider themselves as the ministers of the gods, and the horses, as privy to the divine will. Another kind of divination, by which they explore the event of momentous wars, is to oblige a prisoner, taken by any means whatsoever from the nation with whom they are at variance, to fight with a picked man of their own, each with his own country's arms; and, according as the victory falls, they presage success to the one or to the other party.[69]

11. On affairs of smaller moment, the chiefs consult; on those of greater importance, the whole community; yet with this circumstance, that what is referred to the decision of the people, is first maturely discussed by the chiefs[70]. They assemble, unless upon some sudden emergency, on stated days, either at the new or full moon, which they account the most auspicious season for beginning any enterprise. Nor do they, in their computation of time, reckon, like us, by the number of days, but of nights. In this way they arrange their business; in this way they fix their appointments; so that, with them, the night seems to lead the day[71]. An inconvenience

---

69 Montesquieu finds in this custom the origin of the duel, and of knight-errantry.

70 This remarkable passage, so curious in political history, is commented on by Montesquieu, in his Spirit of Laws. vi 11. That celebrated author expresses his surprise at the existence of such a balance between liberty and authority in the forests of Germany; and traces the origin of the English constitution from this source. Tacitus again mentions the German form of government in his Annals, iv. 33.

71 The high antiquity of this made of reckoning appears from the Book of Genesis. "The evening and the morning were the first day." The Gauls, we

produced by their liberty is, that they do not all assemble at a stated time, as if it were in obedience to a command; but two or three days are lost in the delays of convening. When they all think fit[72], they sit down armed[73]. Silence is proclaimed by the priests, who have on this occasion a coercive power. Then the king, or chief, and such others as are conspicuous for age, birth, military renown, or eloquence, are heard; and gain attention rather from their ability to persuade, than their authority to command. If a proposal displease, the assembly reject it by an inarticulate murmur; if it prove agreeable, they clash their javelins[74]; for the most honorable expression of assent among them is the sound of arms.

12. Before this council, it is likewise allowed to exhibit accusations, and to prosecute capital offences. Punishments are varied according to the nature of the crime. Traitors and deserters

---

are informed by Caesar, "assert that, according to the tradition of their Druids, they are all sprung from Father Dis; on which account they reckon every period of time according to the number of nights, not of days; and observe birthdays and the beginnings of months and years in such a manner, that the day seems to follow the night." (Bell. Gall. vi. 18.) The vestiges of this method of computation still appear in the English language, in the terms se'nnight and fort'night.

72 Ut turbae placuit. Doederlein interprets this passage as representing the confused way in which the people took their seats in the national assembly, without reference to order, rank, age, &c. It rather represents, however, that the people, not the chieftains, determined when the business of the council should begin. - White.

73 And in an open plain. Vast heaps of stone still remaining, denote the scenes of these national councils. (See Mallet's Introduct. to Hist. of Denmark.) The English Stonehenge has been supposed a relic of this kind. In these assemblies are seen the origin of those which, under the Merovingian race of French kings, were called the Fields of March; under the Carlovingian, the Fields of May; then, the Plenary Courts of Christmas and Easter; and lastly, the States General.

74 The speech of Civilis was received with this expression of applause. Tacitus, Hist. iv. 15.

are hung upon trees[75]: cowards, dastards[76], and those guilty of unnatural practices[77], are suffocated in mud under a hurdle[78]. This difference of punishment has in view the principle, that villainy should he exposed while it is punished, but turpitude concealed. The penalties annexed to slighter offences[79] are also proportioned to the delinquency. The convicts are fined in horses and cattle[80]:

---

75 Gibbeted alive. Heavy penalties were denounced against those who should take them down, alive or dead. These are particularized in the Salic law.

76 By cowards and dastards, in this passage, are probably meant those who, being summoned to war, refused or neglected to go. Caesar (Bell. Gall. vi. 22) mentions, that those who refused to follow their chiefs to war were considered as deserters and traitors. And, afterwards, the emperor Clothaire made the following edict, preserved in the Lombard law: "Whatever freeman, summoned to the defence of his country by his Count, or his officers, shall neglect to go, and the enemy enter the country to lay it waste, or otherwise damage our liege subjects, he shall incur a capital punishment." As the crimes of cowardice, treachery, and desertion were so odious and ignominious among the Germans, we find by the Salic law, that penalties were annexed to the unjust imputation of them.

77 These were so rare and so infamous among the Germans, that barely calling a person by a name significant of them was severely punished.

78 Incestuous people were buried alive in bogs in Scotland. Pennant's Tour in Scotland, 1772; part i. p. 351; and part ii. p. 421.

79 Among these slighter offences, however, were reckoned homicide, adultery, theft, and many others of a similar kind. This appears from the laws of the Germans, and from a subsequent passage of Tacitus himself.

80 These were at that time the only riches of the country, as was already observed in this treatise. Afterwards gold and silver became plentiful: hence all the mulcts required by the Salic law are pecuniary. Money, however, still bore a fixed proportion to cattle; as appears from the Saxon law (Tit. xviii.): "The Solidus is of two kinds; one contains two tremisses, that is, a beeve of twelve months, or a sheep with its lamb; the other, three tremisses, or a beeve of sixteen months. Homicide is compounded for by the lesser solidus; other crimes by the greater." The Saxons had their Weregeld, - the Scotch their Cro, Galnes, and Kelchin, - and the Welsh their Gwerth, and Galanus, or compensations for injuries; and cattle were likewise the usual fine. Vide Pennant's Tour in Wales of 1773, pp. 273, 274.

part of the mulct[81] goes to the king or state; part to the injured person, or his relations. In the same assemblies chiefs[82] are also elected, to administer justice through the cantons and districts. A hundred companions, chosen from the people, attended upon each of them, to assist them as well with their advice as their authority.

13. The Germans transact no business, public or private, without being armed[83]: but it is not customary for any person to assume arms till the state has approved his ability to use them. Then, in the midst of the assembly, either one of the chiefs, or the father, or a relation, equips the youth with a shield and javelin[84]. These are to

---

81 This mulct is frequently in the Salic law called "fred," that is, peace; because it was paid to the king or state, as guardians of the public peace.

82 A brief account of the civil economy of the Germans will here be useful. They were divided into nations; of which some were under a regal government, others a republican. The former had kings, the latter chiefs. Both in kingdoms and republics, military affairs were under the conduct of the generals. The nations were divided into cantons; each of which was superintended by a chief, or count, who administered justice in it. The cantons were divided into districts or hundreds, so called because they contained a hundred vills or townships. In each hundred was a companion, or centenary, chosen from the people, before whom small causes were tried. Before the count, all causes, as well great as small, were amenable. The centenaries are called companions by Tacitus, after the custom of the Romans; among whom the titles of honor were, Caesar, the Legatus or Lieutenant of Caesar, and his comites, or companions. The courts of justice were held in the open air, on a rising ground, beneath the shade of an oak, elm, or some other large tree.

83 Even judges were armed on the seat of justice. The Romans, on the contrary, never went armed but when actually engaged in military service.

84 These are the rudiments of the famous institution of chivalry. The sons of kings appear to have received arms from foreign princes. Hence, when Audoin, after overcoming the Gepidae, was requested by the Lombards to dine with his son Alboin, his partner in the victory, he refused; for, says he, "you know it is not customary with us for a king's son to dine with his father, until he has received arms from the king of another country." - Warnefrid, De gestis Langobardorum, i. 23.

them the manly gown[85]; this is the first honor conferred on youth: before this they are considered as part of a household; afterwards, of the state. The dignity of chieftain is bestowed even on mere lads, whose descent is eminently illustrious, or whose fathers have performed signal services to the public; they are associated, however, with those of mature strength, who have already been declared capable of service; nor do they blush to be seen in the rank of companions[86]. For the state of companionship itself has its several degrees, determined by the judgment of him whom they follow; and there is a great emulation among the companions, which shall possess the highest place in the favor of their chief; and among the chiefs, which shall excel in the number and valor of his companions. It is their dignity, their strength, to be always surrounded with a large body of select youth, an ornament in peace, a bulwark in war. And not in his own country alone, but among the neighboring states, the fame and glory of each chief consists in being distinguished for the number and bravery of his companions. Such chiefs are courted by embassies; distinguished by presents; and often by their reputation alone decide a war.

14. In the field of battle, it is disgraceful for the chief to be

---

85 An allusion to the toga virilis of the Romans. The German youth were presented with the shield and spear probably at twelve or fifteen years of age. This early initiation into the business of arms gave them that warlike character for which they were so celebrated. Thus, Seneca (Epist. 46) says, "A native of Germany brandishes, while yet a boy, his slender javelin." And again (in his book on Anger, i. 11), "Who are braver than the Germans? - who more impetuous in the charge? - who fonder of arms, in the use of which they are born and nourished, which are their only care? - who more inured to hardships, insomuch that for the most part they provide no covering for their bodies, no retreat against the perpetual severity of the climate?"

86 Hence it seems that these noble lads were deemed principes in rank, yet had their position among the comites only. The German word Gesell is peculiarly appropriated to these comrades in arms. So highly were they esteemed in Germany, that for killing or hurting them a fine was exacted treble to that for other freemen.

surpassed in valor; it is disgraceful for the companions not to equal their chief; but it is reproach and infamy during a whole succeeding life to retreat from the field surviving him[87]. To aid, to protect him; to place their own gallant actions to the account of his glory, is their first and most sacred engagement. The chiefs fight for victory; the companions for their chief. If their native country be long sunk in peace and inaction, many of the young nobles repair to some other state then engaged in war. For, besides that repose is unwelcome to their race, and toils and perils afford them a better opportunity of distinguishing themselves; they are unable, without war and violence, to maintain a large train of followers. The companion requires from the liberality of his chief, the warlike steed, the bloody and conquering spear: and in place of pay, he expects to be supplied with a table, homely indeed, but plentiful[88]. The funds for this munificence must be found in war and rapine; nor are they so easily persuaded to cultivate the earth, and await the produce of the seasons, as to challenge the foe, and expose themselves to wounds; nay, they even think it base and spiritless to earn by sweat what they might purchase with blood.

15. During the intervals of war, they pass their time less in hunting than in a sluggish repose[89], divided between sleep and the

---

87 Hence, when Chonodomarus, king of the Alamanni, was taken prisoner by the Romans, "his companions, two hundred in number, and three friends peculiarly attached to him, thinking it infamous to survive their prince, or not to die for him, surrendered themselves to be put in bonds." - Ammianus Marcellinus, xvi. 13.

88 Hence Montesquieu (Spirit of Laws, xxx, 3) justly derives the origin of vassalage. At first, the prince gave to his nobles arms and provision: as avarice advanced, money, and then lands, were required, which from benefices became at length hereditary possessions, and were called fiefs. Hence the establishment of the feudal system.

89 Caesar, with less precision, says, "The Germans pass their whole lives in hunting and military exercises." (Bell. Gall, vi. 21.) The picture drawn by Tacitus is more consonant to the genius of a barbarous people: besides that, hunting being the employment but of a few months of the year, a greater part

table. All the bravest of the warriors, committing the care of the house, the family affairs, and the lands, to the women, old men, and weaker part of the domestics, stupefy themselves in inaction: so wonderful is the contrast presented by nature, that the same persons love indolence, and hate tranquillity![90] It is customary for the several states to present, by voluntary and individual contributions[91], cattle or grain[92] to their chiefs; which are accepted as honorary gifts, while they serve as necessary supplies[93]. They are peculiarly pleased with presents from neighboring nations, offered not only by individuals, but by the community at large; such as fine horses, heavy armor, rich housings, and gold chains. We have now taught them also to accept of money.[94]

---

must necessarily be passed in indolence by those who had no other occupation. In this circumstance, and those afterwards related, the North American savages exactly agree with the ancient Germans.

90 This apparent contradiction is, however, perfectly agreeable to the principles of human nature. Among people governed by impulse more than reason, everything is in the extreme: war and peace; motion and rest; love and hatred; none are pursued with moderation.

91 These are the rudiments of tributes; though the contributions here spoken of were voluntary, and without compulsion. The origin of exchequers is pointed out above, where "part of the mulct" is said to be "paid to the king or state." Taxation was taught the Germans by the Romans, who levied taxes upon them.

92 So, in after-times, when tributes were customary, 500 oxen or cows were required annually from the Saxons by the French kings Clothaire I. and Pepin. (See Eccard, tom. i. pp. 84, 480.) Honey, corn, and other products of the earth, were likewise received in tribute. (Ibid. p. 392.)

93 For the expenses of war, and other necessities of state, and particularly the public entertainments. Hence, besides the Steora, or annual tribute, the Osterstuopha, or Easter cup, previous to the public assembly of the Field of March, was paid to the French kings.

94 This was a dangerous lesson, and in the end proved ruinous to the Roman empire. Herodian says of the Germans in his time, "They are chiefly to be prevailed upon by bribes; being fond of money, and continually selling peace to the Romans for gold." - Lib. vi. 139.

16. It is well known that none of the German nations inhabit cities[95]; or even admit of contiguous settlements. They dwell scattered and separate, as a spring, a meadow, or a grove may chance to invite them. Their villages are laid out, not like ours in rows of adjoining buildings; but every one surrounds his house with a vacant space[96], either by way of security against fire[97], or through ignorance of the art of building. For, indeed, they are unacquainted with the use of mortar and tiles; and for every purpose employ rude unshapen timber, fashioned with no regard to pleasing the eye. They bestow more than ordinary pains in coating certain parts of their buildings with a kind of earth, so pure and shining that it gives the appearance of painting. They also dig subterraneous caves[98], and cover them over with a great quantity of dung. These they use as winter-retreats, and granaries; for they preserve a moderate temperature; and upon an invasion, when the open country is plundered, these recesses remain unviolated,

---

95 This custom was of long duration; for there is not the mention of a single city in Ammianus Marcellinus, who wrote on the wars of the Romans in Germany. The names of places in Ptolemy (ii. 11) are not, therefore, those of cities, but of scattered villages. The Germans had not even what we should call towns, notwithstanding Caesar asserts the contrary.

96 The space surrounding the house, and fenced in by hedges, was that celebrated Salic land, which descended to the male line, exclusively of the female.

97 The danger of fire was particularly urgent in time of war; for, as Caesar informs us, these people were acquainted with a method of throwing red-hot clay bullets from slings, and burning javelins, on the thatch of houses. (Bell. Gall. v. 42.)

98 Thus likewise Mela (ii. 1), concerning the Sarmatians: "On account of the length and severity of their winters, they dwell under ground, either in natural or artificial caverns." At the time that Germany was laid waste by a forty years' war, Kircher saw many of the natives who, with their flocks, herds, and other possessions, took refuge in the caverns of the highest mountains. For many other curious particulars concerning these and other subterranean caves, see his Mundus Subterraneus, viii. 3, p. 100. In Hungary, at this day, corn is commonly stored in subterranean chambers.

either because the enemy is ignorant of them, or because he will not trouble himself with the search.[99]

17. The clothing common to all is a sagum[100] fastened by a clasp, or, in want of that, a thorn. With no other covering, they pass whole days on the hearth, before the fire. The more wealthy are distinguished by a vest, not flowing loose, like those of the Sarmatians and Parthians, but girt close, and exhibiting the shape of every limb. They also wear the skins of beasts, which the people near the borders are less curious in selecting or preparing than the more remote inhabitants, who cannot by commerce procure other clothing. These make choice of particular skins, which they variegate with spots, and strips of the furs of marine animals[101], the produce of the exterior ocean, and seas to us unknown[102]. The dress of the women does not differ from that of the men; except that they more frequently wear linen[103], which they stain with

---

99 Near Newbottle, the seat of the Marquis of Lothian, are some subterraneous apartments and passages cut out of the live rock, which had probably served for the same purposes of winter-retreats and granaries as those dug by the ancient Germans. Pennant's Tour in 1769, 4to, p.63.

100 This was a kind of mantle of a square form, called also rheno. Thus Caesar (Bell. Gall. vi. 21): "They use skins for clothing, or the short rhenones, and leave the greatest part of the body naked." Isidore (xix. 23) describes the rhenones as "garments covering the shoulders and breast, as low as the navel, so rough and shaggy that they are impenetrable to rain." Mela (iii. 3), speaking of the Germans, says, "The men are clothed only with the sagum, or the bark of trees, even in the depth of winter."

101 All savages are fond of variety of colors; hence the Germans spotted their furs with the skins of other animals, of which those here mentioned were probably of the seal kind. This practice is still continued with regard to the ermine, which is spotted with black lamb's-skin.

102 The Northern Sea, and Frozen Ocean.

103 Pliny testifies the same thing; and adds, that "the women beyond the Rhine are not acquainted with any more elegant kind of clothing." - xix. 1.

purple[104]; and do not lengthen their upper garment into sleeves, but leave exposed the whole arm, and part of the breast.

18. The matrimonial bond is, nevertheless, strict and severe among them; nor is there anything in their manners more commendable than this[105]. Almost singly among the barbarians, they content themselves with one wife; a very few of them excepted, who, not through incontinence, but because their alliance is solicited on account of their rank[106], practise polygamy. The wife does not bring a dowry to her husband, but receives one from him[107]. The parents and relations assemble, and pass their approbation on the presents - presents not adapted to please a female taste, or decorate the bride; but oxen, a caparisoned steed, a shield, spear, and sword. By virtue of these, the wife is espoused; and she in her turn makes a present of some arms to her husband. This they consider as the firmest bond of union; these, the sacred mysteries, the conjugal deities. That the woman may not think herself excused from exertions of fortitude, or exempt from the

---

104 Not that rich and costly purple in which the Roman nobility shone, but some ordinary material, such as the vaccinium, which Pliny says was used by the Gauls as a purple dye for the garments of the slaves, (xvi. 18.)

105 The chastity of the Germans, and their strict regard to the laws of marriage, are witnessed by all their ancient codes of law. The purity of their manners in this respect afforded a striking contrast to the licentiousness of the Romans in the decline of the empire, and is exhibited in this light by Salvian, in his treatise De Gubernatione Dei, lib. vii.

106 Thus we find in Caesar (Bell. Gall. i. 53) that Ariovistus had two wives. Others had more. This indulgence proved more difficult to abolish, as it was considered as a mark of opulence, and an appendage of nobility.

107 The Germans purchased their wives, as appears from the following clauses in the Saxon law concerning marriage: "A person who espouses a wife shall pay to her parents 300 solidi (about 180_l._ sterling); but if the marriage be without the consent of the parents, the damsel, however, consenting, he shall pay 600 solidi. If neither the parents nor damsel consent, that is, if she be carried off by violence, he shall pay 300 solidi to the parents, and 340 to the damsel, and restore her to her parents."

casualties of war, she is admonished by the very ceremonial of her marriage, that she comes to her husband as a partner in toils and dangers; to suffer and to dare equally with him, in peace and in war: this is indicated by the yoked oxen, the harnessed steed, the offered arms. Thus she is to live; thus to die. She receives what she is to return inviolate[108] and honored to her children; what her daughters-in-law are to receive, and again transmit to her grandchildren.

19. They live, therefore, fenced around with chastity[109]; corrupted by no seductive spectacles[110], no convivial incitements. Men and women are alike unacquainted with clandestine correspondence. Adultery is extremely rare among so numerous a people. Its punishment is instant, and at the pleasure of the husband. He cuts off the hair[111] of the offender, strips her, and in presence of her relations expels her from his house, and pursues her with stripes through the whole village[112]. Nor is any indulgence

---

108 Thus in the Saxon law, concerning dowries, it is said: "The Ostfalii and Angrarii determine, that if a woman have male issue, she is to possess the dower she received in marriage during her life, and transmit it to her sons."

109 Ergo septae pudicitiâ agunt. Some editions have septâ pudicitiâ. This would imply, however, rather the result of the care and watchfulness of their husbands; whereas it seems the object of Tacitus to show that this their chastity was the effect of innate virtue, and this is rather expressed by septae pudicitiâ, which is the reading of the Arundelian MS.

110 Seneca speaks with great force and warmth on this subject: "Nothing is so destructive to morals as loitering at public entertainments; for vice more easily insinuates itself into the heart when softened by pleasure. What shall I say! I return from them more covetous ambitious, and luxurious." - Epist. vii.

111 The Germans had a great regard for the hair, and looked upon cutting it off as a heavy disgrace; so that this was made a punishment for certain crimes, and was resented as an injury if practised upon an innocent person.

112 From an epistle of St. Boniface, archbishop of Mentz, to Ethelbald, king of England, we learn that among the Saxons the women themselves inflicted the punishment for violated chastity; "In ancient Saxony (now Westphalia), if a virgin pollute her father's house, or a married woman prove false to her

shown to a prostitute. Neither beauty, youth, nor riches can procure her a husband: for none there looks on vice with a smile, or calls mutual seduction the way of the world. Still more exemplary is the practice of those states[113] in which none but virgins marry, and the expectations and wishes of a wife are at once brought to a period. Thus, they take one husband as one body and one life; that no thought, no desire, may extend beyond him; and he may be loved not only as their husband, but as their marriage[114]. To limit the increase of children[115], or put to death any of the later progeny[116] is accounted infamous: and good habits have there more influence than good laws elsewhere.[117]

---

vows, sometimes she is forced to put an end to her own life by the halter, and over the ashes of her burned body her seducer is hanged: sometimes a troop of females assembling lead her through the circumjacent villages, lacerating her body, stripped to the girdle, with rods and knives; and thus, bloody and full of minute wounds, she is continually met by new tormenters, who in their zeal for chastity do not quit her till she is dead, or scarcely alive, in order to inspire a dread of such offences." See Michael Alford's Annales Ecclesiae Anglo-Saxon., and Eccard.

113 A passage in Valerius Maximus renders it probable that the Cimbrian states were of this number: "The wives of the Teutones besought Marius, after his victory, that he would deliver them as a present to the Vestal virgins; affirming that they should henceforth, equally with themselves, abstain from the embraces of the other sex. This request not being granted, they all strangled themselves the ensuing night." - Lib. vi. 1.3.

114 Among the Heruli, the wife was expected to hang herself at once at the grave of her husband, if she would not live in perpetual infamy.

115 This expression may signify as well the murder of young children, as the procurement of abortion; both which crimes were severely punished by the German laws.

116 Quemquam ex agnatis. By agnati generally in Roman law were meant relations by the father's side; here it signifies children born after there was already an heir to the name and property of the father.

117 Justin has a similar thought concerning the Scythians: "Justice is cultivated by the dispositions of the people, not by the laws." (ii. 2.) How inefficacious the good laws here alluded to by Tacitus were in preventing enormities among the

20. In every house the children grow up, thinly and meanly clad[118], to that bulk of body and limb which we behold with wonder. Every mother suckles her own children, and does not deliver them into the hands of servants and nurses. No indulgence distinguishes the young master from the slave. They lie together amidst the same cattle, upon the same ground, till age[119] separates, and valor marks out, the free-born. The youths partake late of the pleasures of love[120], and hence pass the age of puberty unexhausted: nor are the virgins hurried into marriage; the same maturity, the same full

---

Romans, appears from the frequent complaints of the senators, and particularly of Minucius Felix; "I behold you, exposing your babes to the wild beasts and birds, or strangling the unhappy wretches with your own hands. Some of you, by means of drugs, extinguish the newly-formed man within your bowels, and thus commit parricide on your offspring before you bring them into the world." (Octavius, c. 30.) So familiar was this practice grown at Rome, that the virtuous Pliny apologises for it, alleging that "the great fertility of some women may require such a licence." - xxix. 4, 37.

118 Nudi ac sordidi does not mean "in nakedness and filth," as most translators have supposed. Personal filth is inconsistent with the daily practice of bathing mentioned c. 22; and nudus does not necessarily imply absolute nakedness (see note 4, p. 293).

119 This age appears at first to have been twelve years; for then a youth became liable to the penalties of law. Thus in the Salic law it is said, "If a child under twelve commit a fault, 'fred,' or a mulct, shall not be required of him." Afterwards the term was fifteen years of age. Thus in the Ripuary law, "A child under fifteen shall not be responsible." Again, "If a man die, or be killed, and leave a son; before he have completed his fifteenth year, he shall neither prosecute a cause, nor be called upon to answer in a suit: but at this term, he must either answer himself, or choose an advocate. In like manner with regard to the female sex." The Burgundian law provides to the same effect. This then was the term of majority, which in later times, when heavier armor was used, was still longer delayed.

120 This is illustrated by a passage in Caesar (Bell. Gall. vi. 21): "They who are the latest in proving their virility are most commended. By this delay they imagine the stature is increased, the strength improved, and the nerves fortified. To have knowledge of the other sex before twenty years of age, is accounted in the highest degree scandalous."

growth is required: the sexes unite equally matched[121] and robust; and the children inherit the vigor of their parents. Children are regarded with equal affection by their maternal uncles[122] as by their fathers: some even consider this as the more sacred bond of consanguinity, and prefer it in the requisition of hostages, as if it held the mind by a firmer tie, and the family by a more extensive obligation. A person's own children, however, are his heirs and successors; and no wills are made. If there be no children, the next in order of inheritance are brothers, paternal and maternal uncles. The more numerous are a man's relations and kinsmen, the more comfortable is his old age; nor is it here any advantage to be childless[123].

21. It is an indispensable duty to adopt the enmities[124] of a father or relation, as well as their friendships: these, however, are not irreconcilable or perpetual. Even homicide is atoned[125] by a certain fine in cattle and sheep; and the whole family accepts the satisfaction, to the advantage of the public weal, since quarrels are

---

121 Equal not only in age and constitution, but in condition. Many of the German codes of law annex penalties to those of both sexes who marry persons of inferior rank.

122 Hence, in the history of the Merovingian kings of France, so many instances of regard to sisters and their children appear, and so many wars undertaken on their account.

123 The court paid at Rome to rich persons without children, by the Haeredipetae, or legacy-hunters, is a frequent subject of censure and ridicule with the Roman writers.

124 Avengers of blood are mentioned in the law of Moses, Numb. xxxv. 19. In the Roman law also, under the head of "those who on account of unworthiness are deprived of their inheritance," it is pronounced, that "such heirs as are proved to have neglected revenging the testator's death, shall be obliged to restore the entire profits."

125 It was a wise provision, that among this fierce and warlike people, revenge should be commuted for a payment. That this intention might not be frustrated by the poverty of the offender, his whole family were conjointly bound to make compensation.

most dangerous in a free state. No people are more addicted to social entertainments, or more liberal in the exercise of hospitality[126]. To refuse any person whatever admittance under their roof, is accounted flagitious[127]. Every one according to his ability feasts his guest: when his provisions are exhausted, he who was late the host, is now the guide and companion to another hospitable board. They enter the next house uninvited, and are received with equal cordiality. No one makes a distinction with respect to the rights of hospitality, between a stranger and an acquaintance. The departing guest is presented with whatever he may ask for; and with the same freedom a boon is desired in return. They are pleased with presents; but think no obligation incurred either when they give or receive.

22.[128] [Their manner of living with their guest is easy and affable] As soon as they arise from sleep, which they generally protract till late in the day, they bathe, usually in warm water[129], as

---

126 All uncivilized nations agree in this property, which becomes less necessary as a nation improves in the arts of civil life.

127 Convictibus et hospitiis. "Festivities and entertainments." The former word applies to friends and fellow-countrymen; the latter, to those not of the same tribe, and foreigners. Caesar (Bell. Gall. vi. 23) says, "They think it unlawful to offer violence to their guests, who, on whatever occasion they come to them, are protected from injury, and considered as sacred. Every house is open to them, and provision everywhere set before them." Mela (iii. 3) says of the Germans, "They make right consist in force, so that they are not ashamed of robbery: they are only kind to their guests, and merciful to suppliants. The Burgundian law lays a fine of three solidi on every man who refuses his roof or hearth to the coming guest." The Salic law, however, rightly forbids the exercise of hospitality to atrocious criminals; laying a penalty on the person who shall harbor one who has dug up or despoiled the dead? till he has made satisfaction to the relations.

128 The clause here put within brackets is probably misplaced; since it does not connect well either with what goes before or what follows.

129 The Russians are at present the most remarkable among the northern nations for the use of warm bathing. Some of the North American tribes also

cold weather chiefly prevails there. After bathing they take their meal, each on a distinct seat, and a a separate table[130]. Then they proceed, armed, to business, and not less frequently to convivial parties, in which it is no disgrace to pass days and nights, without intermission, in drinking. The frequent quarrels that arise amongst them, when intoxicated, seldom terminate in abusive language, but more frequently in blood[131]. In their feasts, they generally deliberate on the reconcilement of enemies, on family alliances, on the appointment of chiefs, and finally on peace and war; conceiving that at no time the soul is more opened to sincerity, or warmed to heroism. These people, naturally void of artifice or disguise, disclose the most secret emotions of their hearts in the freedom of festivity. The minds of all being thus displayed without reserve, the subjects of their deliberation are again canvassed the next day[132]; and each time has its advantages. They consult when unable to dissemble; they determine when not liable to mistake.

23. Their drink is a liquor prepared from barley or wheat[133]

---

have their hypocausts, or stoves.

130 Eating at separate tables is generally an indication of voracity. Traces of it may be found in Homer, and other writers who have described ancient manners. The same practice has also been observed among the people of Otaheite; who occasionally devour vast quantities of food.

131 The following article in the Salic law shows at once the frequency of these bloody quarrels, and the laudable endeavors of the legislature to restrain them; - "If at a feast where there are four or five men in company, one of them be killed, the rest shall either convict one as the offender, or shall jointly pay the composition for his death. And this law shall extend to seven persons present at an entertainment."

132 The same custom is related by Herodotus, i. p. 66, as prevailing among the Persians.

133 Of this liquor, beer or ale, Pliny speaks in the following passage: "The western nations have their intoxicating liquor, made of steeped grain. The Egyptians also invented drinks of the same kind. Thus drunkenness is a stranger in no part of the world; for these liquors are taken pure, and not diluted as wine is. Yet, surely, the Earth thought she was producing corn. Oh, the

brought by fermentation to a certain resemblance of wine. Those who border on the Rhine also purchase wine. Their food is simple; wild fruits, fresh venison[134], or coagulated milk[135]. They satisfy hunger without seeking the elegances and delicacies of the table. Their thirst for liquor is not quenched with equal moderation. If their propensity to drunkenness be gratified to the extent of their wishes, intemperance proves as effectual in subduing them as the force of arms[136].

24. They have only one kind of public spectacle, which is exhibited in every company. Young men, who make it their diversion, dance naked amidst drawn swords and presented spears. Practice has conferred skill at this exercise; and skill has given grace; but they do not exhibit for hire or gain: the only reward of this pastime, though a hazardous one, is the pleasure of the spectators. What is extraordinary, they play at dice, when sober, as a serious business: and that with such a desperate venture of gain

---

wonderful sagacity of our vices! we have discovered how to render even water intoxicating." - xiv. 22.

134 Mela says, "Their manner of living is so rude and savage, that they eat even raw flesh; either fresh killed, or softened by working with their hands and feet, after it has grown stiff in the hides of tame or wild animals." (iii. 3.) Florus relates that the ferocity of the Cimbri was mitigated by their feeding on bread and dressed meat, and drinking wine, in the softest tract of Italy. - iii. 3.

135 This must not be understood to have been cheese; although Caesar says of the Germans, "Their diet chiefly consists of milk, cheese and flesh." (Bell. Gall. vi. 22.) Pliny, who was thoroughly acquainted with the German manners, says more accurately, "It is surprising that the barbarous nations who live on milk should for so many ages have been ignorant of, or have rejected, the preparation of cheese; especially since they thicken their milk into a pleasant tart substance, and a fat butter: this is the scum of milk, of a thicker consistence than what is called the whey. It must not be omitted that it has the properties of oil, and is used as an unguent by all the barbarians, and by us for children." - xi. 41.

136 This policy has been practised by the Europeans with regard to the North American savages, some tribes of which have been almost totally extirpated by it.

or loss, that, when everything else is gone, they set their liberties and persons on the last throw. The loser goes into voluntary servitude; and, though the youngest and strongest, patiently suffers himself to be bound and sold[137]. Such is their obstinacy in a bad practice - they themselves call it honor. The slaves thus acquired are exchanged away in commerce, that the winner may get rid of the scandal of his victory.

25. The rest of their slaves have not, like ours, particular employments in the family allotted them. Each is the master of a habitation and household of his own. The lord requires from him a certain quantity of grain, cattle, or cloth, as from a tenant; and so far only the subjection of the slave extends[138]. His domestic offices are performed by his own wife and children. It is usual to scourge a slave, or punish him with chains or hard labor. They are sometimes killed by their masters; not through severity of chastisement, but

---

137 St. Ambrose has a remarkable passage concerning this spirit of gaming among a barbarous people: - "It is said that the Huns, who continually make war upon other nations, are themselves subject to usurers, with whom they run in debt at play; and that, while they live without laws, they obey the laws of the dice alone; playing when drawn up in line of battle; carrying dice along with their arms, and perishing more by each others' hands than by the enemy. In the midst of victory they submit to become captives, and suffer plunder from their own countrymen, which they know not how to bear from the foe. On this account they never lay aside the business of war, because, when they have lost all their booty by the dice, they have no means of acquiring fresh supplies for play, but by the sword. They are frequently borne away with such a desperate ardor, that, when the loser has given up his arms, the only part of his property which he greatly values, he sets the power over his life at a single cast to the winner or usurer. It is a fact, that a person, known to the Roman emperor, paid the price of a servitude which he had by this means brought upon himself, by suffering death at the command of his master."

138 The condition of these slaves was the same as that of the vassals, or serfs, who a few centuries ago made the great body of the people in every country in Europe. The Germans, in after times, imitating the Romans, had slaves of inferior condition, to whom the name of slave became appropriated; while those in the state of rural vassalage were called lidi.

in the heat of passion, like an enemy; with this difference, that it is done with impunity[139]. Freedmen are little superior to slaves; seldom filling any important office in the family; never in the state, except in those tribes which are under regal government[140]. There, they rise above the free-born, and even the nobles: in the rest, the subordinate condition of the freedmen is a proof of freedom.

26. Lending money upon interest, and increasing it by usury[141], is unknown amongst them: and this ignorance more effectually prevents the practice than a prohibition would do. The lands are occupied by townships[142], in allotments proportional to the number of cultivators; and are afterwards parcelled out among the individuals of the district, in shares according to the rank and condition of each person[143]. The wide extent of plain facilitates

---

139 A private enemy could not be slain with impunity, since a fine was affixed to homicide; but a man might kill his own slave without any punishment. If, however, he killed another person's slave, he was obliged to pay his price to the owner.

140 The amazing height of power and insolence to which freedmen arrived by making themselves subservient to the vices of the prince, is a striking characteristic of the reigns of some of the worst of the Roman emperors.

141 In Rome, on the other hand, the practice of usury was, as our author terms it, "an ancient evil, and a perpetual source of sedition and discord." - Annals, vi. 16.

142 All the copies read per vices, "by turns," or alternately; but the connection seems evidently to require the easy alteration of per vicos, which has been approved by many learned commentators, and is therefore adopted in this translation.

143 Caesar has several particulars concerning this part of German polity. "They are not studious of agriculture, the greater part of their diet consisting of milk, cheese, and flesh; nor has any one a determinate portion of land, his own peculiar property; but the magistrates and chiefs allot every year to tribes and clanships forming communities, as much land, and in such situations, as they think proper, and oblige them to remove the succeeding year. For this practice they assign several reasons: as, lest they should be led, by being accustomed to one spot, to exchange the toils of war for the business of agriculture; lest they should acquire a passion for possessing extensive domains, and the

this partition. The arable lands are annually changed, and a part left fallow; nor do they attempt to make the most of the fertility and plenty of the soil, by their own industry in planting orchards, inclosing meadows, and watering gardens. Corn is the only product required from the earth: hence their year is not divided into so many seasons as ours; for, while they know and distinguish by name Winter, Spring, and Summer, they are unacquainted equally with the appellation and bounty of Autumn[144].

27. Their funerals are without parade[145]. The only circumstance to which they attend, is to burn the bodies of eminent persons with some particular kinds of wood. Neither vestments nor perfumes are heaped upon the pile[146]: the arms of the deceased,

---

more powerful should be tempted to dispossess the weaker; lest they should construct buildings with more art than was necessary to protect them from the inclemencies of the weather; lest the love of money should arise amongst them, the source of faction and dissensions; and in order that the people, beholding their own possessions equal to those of the most powerful, might be retained by the bonds of equity and moderation." - Bell. Gall. vi. 21.

144 The Germans, not planting fruit-trees, were ignorant of the proper products of autumn. They have now all the autumnal fruits of their climate; yet their language still retains a memorial of their ancient deficiencies, in having no term for this season of the year, but one denoting the gathering in of corn alone - Herbst, Harvest.

145 In this respect, as well as many others, the manners of the Germans were a direct contrast to those of the Romans. Pliny mentions a private person, C. Caecilius Claudius Isidorus, who ordered the sum of about 10,000_l._ sterling to be expended in his funeral: and in another place he says, "Intelligent persons asserted that Arabia did not produce such a quantity of spices in a year as Nero burned at the obsequies of his Poppaea." - xxxiii. 10, and xii. 18.

146 The following lines of Lucan, describing the last honors paid by Cornelia to the body of Pompey the Great, happily illustrate the customs here referred to: -
Collegit vestes, miserique insignia Magni.
Armaque, et impressas auro, quas gesserat olim
Exuvias, pictasque togas, velamina summo
Ter conspecta Jovi, funestoque intulit igni. - Lib. ix. 175.
"There shone his arms, with antique gold inlaid,

and sometimes his horse[147], are given to the flames. The tomb is a mound of turf. They contemn the elaborate and costly honours of monumental structures, as mere burthens to the dead. They soon dismiss tears and lamentations; slowly, sorrow and regret. They think it the women's part to bewail their friends, the men's to remember them.

28. This is the sum of what I have been able to learn concerning the origin and manners of the Germans in general. I now proceed to mention those particulars in which they differ from each other; and likewise to relate what nations have migrated from Germany into Gaul. That great writer, the deified Julius, asserts that the Gauls were formerly the superior people[148]; whence it is probable that some Gallic colonies passed over into Germany: for how small an obstacle would a river be to prevent any nation, as it increased in strength, from occupying or changing settlements as yet lying in common, and unappropriated by the power of

---

There the rich robes which she herself had made,
Robes to imperial Jove in triumph thrice display'd:
The relics of his past victorious days,
Now this his latest trophy serve to raise,
And in one common flame together blaze." - ROWE.

147 Thus in the tomb of Childeric, king of the Franks, were found his spear and sword, and also his horse's head, with a shoe, and gold buckles and housings. A human skull was likewise discovered, which, perhaps, was that of his groom.

148 Caesar's account is as follows: - "There was formerly a time when the Gauls surpassed the Germans in bravery, and made war upon them; and, on account of their multitude of people and scarcity of land, sent colonies beyond the Rhine. The most fertile parts of Germany, adjoining to the Hercynian forest, (which, I observe, was known by report to Eratosthenes and others of the Greeks, and called by them Orcinia,) were accordingly occupied by the Volcae and Tectosages, who settled there. These people still continue in the same settlements, and have a high character as well for the administration of justice as military prowess: and they now remain in the same state of penury and content as the Germans, whose manner of life they have adopted." - Bell. Gall. vi. 24.

monarchies! Accordingly, the tract betwixt the Hercynian forest and the rivers Rhine and Mayne was possessed by the Helvetii[149]: and that beyond, by the Boii[150]; both Gallic tribes. The name of Boiemum still remains, a memorial of the ancient settlement, though its inhabitants are now changed[151]. But whether the Aravisci[152] migrated into Pannonia from the Osi[153], a German nation; or the Osi into Germany from the Aravisci; the language, institutions, and manners of both being still the same, is a matter of uncertainty; for, in their pristine state of equal indigence and equal liberty, the same advantages and disadvantages were common to both sides of the river. The Treveri[154] and Nervii[155] are

---

149 The inhabitants of Switzerland, then extending further than at present, towards Lyons.

150 A nation of Gauls, bordering on the Helvetii, as appears from Strabo and Caesar. After being conquered by Caesar, the Aedui gave them a settlement in the country now called the Bourbonnois. The name of their German colony, Boiemum, is still extant in Bohemia. The aera at which the Helvetii and Boii penetrated into Germany is not ascertained. It seems probable, however, that it was in the reign of Tarquinius Priscus; for at that time, as we are told by Livy, Ambigatus, king of the Bituriges (people of Berry), sent his sister's son Sigovesus into the Hercynian forest, with a colony, in order to exonerate his kingdom which was overpeopled. (Livy, v. 33; et seq.)

151 In the time of Augustus, the Boii, driven from Boiemum by the Marcomanni, retired to Noricum, which from them was called Boioaria, now Bavaria.

152 This people inhabited that part of Lower Hungary now called the Palatinate of Pilis.

153 Towards the end of this treatise, Tacitus seems himself to decide this point, observing that their use of the Pannonian language, and acquiescence in paying tribute, prove the Osi not to be a German nation. They were settled beyond the Marcomanni and Quadi, and occupied the northern part of Transdanubian Hungary; perhaps extending to Silesia, where is a place called Ossen in the duchy of Oels, famous for salt and glass works. The learned Pelloutier, however, contends that the Osi were Germans; but with less probability.

154 The inhabitants of the modern diocese of Treves.

155 Those of Cambresis and Hainault.

ambitious of being thought of German origin; as if the reputation of this descent would distinguish them from the Gauls, whom they resemble in person and effeminacy. The Vangiones, Triboci, and Nemetes[156], who inhabit the bank of the Rhine, are without doubt German tribes. Nor do the Ubii[157], although they have been thought worthy of being made a Roman colony, and are pleased in bearing the name of Agrippinenses from their founder, blush to acknowledge their origin from Germany; from whence they formerly migrated, and for their approved fidelity were settled on the bank of the Rhine, not that they might be guarded themselves, but that they might serve as a guard against invaders.

29. Of all these people, the most famed for valor are the Batavi; whose territories comprise but a small part of the banks of the Rhine, but consist chiefly of an island within it[158]. These were formerly a tribe of the Catti, who, on account of an intestine division, removed to their present settlements, in order to become a part of the Roman empire. They still retain this honor, together with a memorial of their ancient alliance[159]; for they are neither insulted by taxes, nor oppressed by farmers of the revenue. Exempt from fiscal burthens and extraordinary contributions, and kept apart for military use alone, they are reserved, like a magazine of arms, for the purposes of war. The nation of the Mattiaci[160] is

---

156 Those of the dioceses of Worms, Strasburg, and Spires.

157 Those of the diocese of Cologne. The Ubii, migrating from Germany to Gaul, on account of the enmity of the Catti, and their own attachment to the Roman interest, were received under the protection of Marcus Agrippa, in the year of Rome 717. (Strabo, iv. p. 194.) Agrippina, the wife of Claudius and mother of Nero, who was born among them, obtained the settlement of a colony there, which was called after her name.

158 Now the Betuwe, part of the provinces of Holland and Guelderland.

159 Hence the Batavi are termed, in an ancient inscription, "the brothers and friends of the Roman people."

160 This nation inhabited part of the countries now called the Weteraw, Hesse,

under a degree of subjection of the same kind: for the greatness of the Roman people has carried a reverence for the empire beyond the Rhine and the ancient limits. The Mattiaci, therefore, though occupying a settlement and borders[161] on the opposite side of the river, from sentiment and attachment act with us; resembling the Batavi in every respect, except that they are animated with a more vigorous spirit by the soil and air of their own country[162]. I do not reckon among the people of Germany those who occupy the Decumate lands[163], although inhabiting between the Rhine and Danube. Some of the most fickle of the Gauls, rendered daring through indigence, seized upon this district of uncertain property. Afterwards, our boundary line being advanced, and a chain of

---

Isenburg and Fulda. In this territory was Mattium, now Marpurg, and the Fontes Mattiaci, now Wisbaden, near Mentz.

161 The several people of Germany had their respective borders, called marks or marches, which they defended by preserving them in a desert and uncultivated state. Thus Caesar, Bell. Gall. iv 3: - "They think it the greatest honor to a nation, to have as wide an extent of vacant land around their dominions as possible; by which it is indicated, that a great number of neighboring communities are unable to withstand them. On this account, the Suevi are said to have, on one side, a tract of 600 (some learned men think we should read 60) miles desert for their boundaries." In another place Caesar mentions, as an additional reason for this policy, that they think themselves thereby rendered secure from the danger of sudden incursions. (Bell. Gall. vi. 13.)

162 The difference between the low situation and moist air of Batavia, and the high and dry country of the Mattiaci, will sufficiently justify this remark, in the opinion of those who allow anything to the influence of climate.

163 Now Swabia. When the Marcommanni, towards the end of the reign of Augustus, quitting their settlements near the Rhine, migrated to Bohemia, the lands they left vacant were occupied by some unsettled Gauls among the Rauraci and Sequani. They seem to have been called Decumates (Decimated), because the inhabitants, liable to the incursions of the Germans, paid a tithe of their products to be received under the protection of the Romans. Adrian defended them by a rampart, which extended from Neustadt, a town on the Danube near the mouth of the river Altmühl, to the Neckar near Wimpfen; a space of sixty French leagues.

fortified posts established, it became a skirt of the empire, and part of the Roman province[164].

30. Beyond these dwell the Catti[165], whose settlements, beginning from the Hercynian forest, are in a tract of country less open and marshy than those which overspread the other states of Germany; for it consists of a continued range of hills, which gradually become more scattered; and the Hercynian forest[166] both accompanies and leaves behind, its Catti. This nation is distinguished by hardier frames[167], compactness of limb, fierceness of countenance, and superior vigor of mind. For Germans, they have a considerable share of understanding and sagacity; they choose able persons to command, and obey them when chosen; keep their ranks; seize opportunities; restrain impetuous motions; distribute properly the business of the day; intrench themselves against the night; account fortune dubious, and valor only certain; and, what is extremely rare, and only a consequence of discipline,

---

164 Of Upper Germany.

165 The Catti possessed a large territory between the Rhine, Mayne and Sala, and the Hartz forest on this side of the Weser; where are now the countries of Hesse, Thuringia, part of Paderborn, of Fulda, and of Franconia. Learned writers have frequently noted, that what Caesar, Florus and Ptolemy have said of the Suevi, is to be understood of the Catti. Leibnitz supposes the Catti were so called from the active animal which they resemble in name, the German for cat being Catte, or Hessen.

166 Pliny, who was well acquainted with Germany, gives a very striking description of the Hercynian forest: - "The vast trees of the Hercynian forest, untouched for ages, and as old as the world, by their almost immortal destiny exceed common wonders. Not to mention circumstances which would not be credited, it is certain that hills are raised by the repercussion of their meeting roots; and where the earth does not follow them, arches are formed as high as the branches, which, struggling, as it were, with each other, are bent into the form of open gates, so wide, that troops of horse may ride under them." - xvi. 2.

167 Duriora corpora. "Hardier frames;" i.e. than the rest of the Germans. At Hist. ii 32. the Germans, in general, are said to have fluxa corpora; while in c. 4 of this treatise they are described as tantùm ad impetum valida.

depend more upon the general than the army[168]. Their force consists entirely in infantry; who, besides their arms, are obliged to carry tools and provisions. Other nations appear to go to a battle; the Catti, to war. Excursions and casual encounters are rare amongst them. It is, indeed, peculiar to cavalry soon to obtain, and soon to yield, the victory. Speed borders upon timidity; slow movements are more akin to steady valor.

31. A custom followed among the other German nations only by a few individuals, of more daring spirit than the rest, is adopted by general consent among the Catti. From the time they arrive at years of maturity they let their hair and beard grow[169]; and do not divest themselves of this votive badge, the promise of valor, till they have slain an enemy. Over blood and spoils they unveil the countenance, and proclaim that they have at length paid the debt of existence, and have proved themselves worthy of their country and parents. The cowardly and effeminate continue in their squalid disguise. The bravest among them wear also an iron ring[170] (a mark

---

168 Floras, ii. 18, well expresses this thought by the sentence "Tanti exercitus, quanti imperator." "An army is worth so much as its general is."

169 Thus Civilis is said by our author (Hist. iv. 61), to have let his hair and beard grow in consequence of a private vow. Thus too, in Paul Warnefrid's "History of the Lombards," iii. 7, it is related, that "six thousand Saxons who survived the war, vowed that they would never cut their hair, nor shave their beards, till they had been revenged of their enemies, the Suevi." A later instance of this custom is mentioned by Strada (Bell. Belg. vii. p. 344), of William Lume, one of the Counts of Mark, "who bound himself by a vow not to cut his hair till he had revenged the deaths of Egmont and Horn."

170 The iron ring seems to have been a badge of slavery. This custom was revived in later times, but rather with a gallant than a military intention. Thus, in the year 1414, John duke of Bourbon, in order to ingratiate himself with his mistress, vowed, together with sixteen knights and gentlemen, that they would wear, he and the knights a gold ring, the gentlemen a silver one, round their left legs, every Sunday for two years, till they had met with an equal number of knights and gentlemen to contend with them in a tournament. (Vertot, Mém. de l'Acad. des Inscr. tom. ii. p. 596.)

of ignominy in that nation) as a kind of chain, till they have released themselves by the slaughter of a foe. Many of the Catti assume this distinction, and grow hoary under the mark, conspicuous both to foes and friends. By these, in every engagement, the attack is begun: they compose the front line, presenting a new spectacle of terror. Even in peace they do not relax the sternness of their aspect. They have no house, land, or domestic cares: they are maintained by whomsoever they visit: lavish of another's property, regardless of their own; till the debility of age renders them unequal to such a rigid course of military virtue[171].

32. Next to the Catti, on the banks of the Rhine, where, now settled in its channel, it is become a sufficient boundary, dwell the Usipii and Tencteri[172]. The latter people, in addition to the usual military reputation, are famed for the discipline of their cavalry; nor is the infantry of the Catti in higher estimation than the horse of the Tencteri. Their ancestors established it, and are imitated by posterity. Horsemanship is the sport of their children, the point of emulation of their youth, and the exercise in which they persevere to old age. Horses are bequeathed along with the domestics, the household gods, and the rights of inheritance: they do not, however, like other things, go to the eldest son, but to the bravest and most warlike.

---

171 It was this nation of Catti, which, about 150 years afterwards, uniting with the remains of the Cherusci on this side the Weser, the Attuarii, Sicambri, Chamavi, Bructeri, and Chauci, entered into the Francic league, and, conquering the Romans, seized upon Gaul. From them are derived the name, manners, and laws of the French.

172 These two tribes, united by a community of wars and misfortunes, had formerly been driven from the settlements on the Rhine a little below Mentz. They then, according to Caesar (Bell. Gall. iv. 1, et seq.), occupied the territories of the Menapii on both sides the Rhine. Still proving unfortunate, they obtained the lands of the Sicambri, who, in the reign of Augustus, were removed on this side the Rhine by Tiberius: these were the present counties of Berg, Mark, Lippe, and Waldeck; and the bishopric of Paderborn.

33. Contiguous to the Tencteri were formerly the Bructeri[173]; but report now says that the Chamavi and Angrivarii[174], migrating into their country, have expelled and entirely extirpated them[175], with the concurrence of the neighboring nations, induced either by hatred of their arrogance[176], love of plunder, or the favor of the gods towards the Romans. For they even gratified us with the spectacle of a battle, in which above sixty thousand Germans were slain, not by Roman arms, but, what was still grander, by mutual hostilities, as it were for our pleasure and entertainment[177]. May

---

173 Their settlements were between the rivers Rhine, Lippe (Luppia), and Ems (Amisia), and the province of Friesland; now the countries of Westphalia and Over-Issel. Alting (Notit. German. Infer, p. 20) supposes they derived their name from Broeken, or Bruchen, marshes, on account of their frequency in that tract of country.

174 Before this migration, the Chamavi were settled on the Ems, where at present are Lingen and Osnaburg; the Angrivarii, on the Weser (Visurgis), where are Minden and Schawenburg. A more ancient migration of the Chamavi to the banks of the Rhine is cursorily mentioned by Tacitus, Annal. xiii. 55. The Angrivarii were afterwards called Angrarii, and became part of the Saxon nation.

175 They were not so entirely extirpated that no relics of them remained. They were even a conspicuous part of the Francic league, as before related. Claudian also, in his panegyric on the fourth consulate of Honorius, v. 450, mentions them.
   Venit accola sylvae
   Bructerus Hercyniae.
   "The Bructerian, borderer on the Hercynian forest, came."
   After their expulsion, they settled, according to Eccard, between Cologne and Hesse.

176 The Bructeri were under regal government, and maintained many wars against the Romans. Hence their arrogance and power. Before they were destroyed by their countrymen, Vestricius Spurinna terrified them into submission without an action, and had on that account a triumphal statue decreed him. Pliny the younger mentions this fact, book ii. epist. 7.

177 An allusion to gladiatorial spectacles. This slaughter happened near the

the nations retain and perpetuate, if not an affection for us, at least an animosity against each other! since, while the fate of the empire is thus urgent[178], fortune can bestow no higher benefit upon us, than the discord of our enemies.

34. Contiguous to the Angrivarii and Chamavi backwards lie the Dulgibini, Chasauri[179], and other nations less known[180]. In front, the Frisii[181] succeed; who are distinguished by the appellations of Greater and Lesser, from their proportional power. The settlements of both stretch along the border of the Rhine to the ocean; and include, besides, vast lakes[182], which have been navigated by

---

canal of Drusus, where the Roman guard on the Rhine could be spectators of the battle. The account of it came to Rome in the first year of Trajan.

178 As this treatise was written in the reign of Trajan, when the affairs of the Romans appeared unusually prosperous, some critics have imagined that Tacitus wrote vigentibus, "flourishing," instead of urgentibus, "urgent." But it is sufficiently evident, from other passages, that the causes which were operating gradually, but surely, to the destruction of the Roman empire, did not escape the penetration of Tacitus, even when disguised by the most flattering appearances. The common reading is therefore, probably, right. - Aikin.

179 These people first resided near the head of the Lippe; and then removed to the settlements of the Chamavi and Angrivarii, who had expelled the Bructeri. They appear to have been the same with those whom Velleius Paterculus, ii. 105, calls the Attuarii, and by that name they entered into the Francic league. Strabo calls them Chattuarii.

180 Namely, the Ansibarii and Tubantes. The Ansibarii or Amsibarii are thought by Alting to have derived their name from their neighborhood to the river Ems (Amisia); and the. Tubantes, from their frequent change of habitation, to have been called Tho Benten. or the wandering troops, and to have dwelt where now is Drente in Over-Issel. Among these nations, Furstenburg (Monum. Paderborn.) enumerates the Ambrones, borderers upon the river Ambrus, now Emmeren.

181 The Frieslanders. The lesser Frisii were settled on this side, the greater, on the other, of the Flevum (Zuyderzee).

182 In the time of the Romans this country was covered by vast meres, or lakes; which were made still larger by frequent inundations of the sea. Of these, one so late as 1530 overwhelmed seventy-two villages; and another, still more terrible,

Roman fleets. We have even explored the ocean itself on that side; and fame reports that columns of Hercules[183] are still remaining on that coast; whether it be that Hercules was ever there in reality, or that whatever great and magnificent is anywhere met with is, by common consent, ascribed to his renowned name. The attempt of Drusus Germanicus[184] to make discoveries in these parts was sufficiently daring; but the ocean opposed any further inquiry into itself and Hercules. After a while no one renewed the attempt; and it was thought more pious and reverential to believe the actions of the gods, than to investigate them.

35. Hitherto we have traced the western side of Germany. It turns from thence with a vast sweep to the north: and first occurs the country of the Chauci[185], which, though it begins immediately

---

in 1569, laid under water great part of the sea-coast of Holland, and almost all Friesland, in which alone 20,000 persons were drowned.

183 Wherever the land seemed to terminate, and it appeared impossible to proceed further, maritime nations have feigned pillars of Hercules. Those celebrated by the Frisians must have been at the extremity of Friesland, and not in Sweden and the Cimmerian promontory, as Rudbeck supposes.

184 Drusus, the brother of Tiberius, and father of Germanicus, imposed a tribute on the Frisians, as mentioned in the Annals, iv. 72, and performed other eminent services in Germany; himself styled Germanicus.

185 The Chauci extended along the seacoast from the Ems to the Elbe (Albis); whence they bordered on all the fore-mentioned nations, between which and the Cherusci they came round to the Catti. The Chauci were distinguished into Greater and Lesser. The Greater, according to Ptolemy, inhabited the country between the Weser and the Elbe; the Lesser, that between the Weser and Ems; but Tacitus (Annals xi. 19) seems to reverse this order. Alting supposes the Chauci had their name from Kauken, signifying persons eminent for valor and fidelity, which agrees with the character Tacitus gives them. Others derive it from Kauk, an owl, with a reference to the enmity of that animal to cats (Catti). Others, from Kaiten, daws, of which there are great numbers on their coast. Pliny has admirably described the country and manners of the maritime Chauci, in his account of people who live without any trees or fruit-bearing vegetables: - "In the North are the nations of Chauci, who are divided into Greater and Lesser. Here, the ocean, having a prodigious flux and reflux twice in the space of

85

from Frisia, and occupies part of the seashore, yet stretches so far as to border on all the nations before mentioned, till it winds round so as to meet the territories of the Catti. This immense tract is not only possessed, but filled by the Chauci; a people the noblest of the Germans, who choose to maintain their greatness by justice rather than violence. Without ambition, without ungoverned desires, quiet and retired, they provoke no wars, they are guilty of no rapine or plunder; and it is a principal proof of their power and bravery, that the superiority they possess has not been acquired by unjust means. Yet all have arms in readiness[186]; and, if necessary, an army is soon raised: for they abound in men and horses, and maintain their military reputation even in inaction.

36. Bordering on the Chauci and Catti are the Cherusci[187]; who,

---

every day and night, rolls over an immense tract, leaving it a matter of perpetual doubt whether it is part of the land or sea. In this spot, the wretched natives, occupying either the tops of hills, or artificial mounds of turf, raised out of reach of the highest tides, build their small cottages; which appear like sailing vessels when the water covers the circumjacent ground, and like wrecks when it has retired. Here from their huts they pursue the fish, continually flying from them with the waves. They do not, like their neighbors, possess cattle, and feed on milk; nor have they a warfare to maintain against wild beasts, for every fruit of the earth is far removed from them. With flags and seaweed they twist cordage for their fishing-nets. For fuel they use a kind of mud, taken up by hand, and dried, rather in the wind than the sun: with this earth they heat their food, and warm their bodies, stiffened by the rigorous north. Their only drink is rain-water collected in ditches at the thresholds of their doors. Yet this miserable people, if conquered to-day by the Roman arms, would call themselves slaves. Thus it is that fortune spares many to their own punishment." - Hist. Nat. xvi. 1.

186 On this account, fortified posts were established by the Romans to restrain the Chauci; who by Lucan are called Cayci in the following passage:

Et vos crinigeros bellis arcere Caycos
Oppositi. - Phars. i. 463.
"You, too, tow'rds Rome advance, ye warlike band,
That wont the shaggy Cauci to withstand." - ROWE

187 The Cherusci, at that time, dwelt between the Weser and the Elbe, where now are Luneburg, Brunswick, and part of the Marche of Brandenburg on this

for want of an enemy, long cherished a too lasting and enfeebling peace: a state more flattering than secure; since the repose enjoyed amidst ambitious and powerful neighbors is treacherous; and when an appeal is made to the sword, moderation and probity are names appropriated by the victors. Thus, the Cherusci, who formerly bore the titles of just and upright, are now charged with cowardice and folly; and the good fortune of the Catti, who subdued them, has grown into wisdom. The ruin of the Cherusci involved that of the Fosi[188], a neighboring tribe, equal partakers of their adversity, although they had enjoyed an inferior share of their prosperity.

37. In the same quarter of Germany, adjacent to the ocean, dwell the Cimbri[189]; a small[190] state at present, but great in

---

side the Elbe. In the reign of Augustus they occupied a more extensive tract; reaching even this side the Weser, as appears from the accounts of the expedition of Drusus given by Dio and Velleius Paterculus: unless, as Dithmar observes, what is said of the Cherusci on this side the Weser relates to the Dulgibini, their dependents. For, according to Strabo, Varus was cut off by the Cherusci, and the people subject to them. The brave actions of Arminius, the celebrated chief of the Cherusci, are related by Tacitus in the 1st and 2nd books of his Annals.

188 Cluver, and several others, suppose the Fosi to have been the same with the ancient Saxons: but, since they bordered on the Cherusci, the opinion of Leibnitz is nearer the truth, that they inhabited the banks of the river Fusa, which enters the Aller (Allera) at Cellae; and were a sort of appendage to the Cherusci, as Hildesheim now is to Brunswick. The name of Saxons is later than Tacitus, and was not known till the reign of Antoninus Pius, at which period they poured forth from the Cimbric Chersonesus, and afterwards, in conjunction with the Angles, seized upon Britain.

189 The name of this people still exists; and the country they inhabited is called the Cimbric Chersonesus, or Peninsula; comprehending Jutland, Sleswig, and Holstein. The renown and various fortune of the Cimbri is briefly, but accurately, related by Mallet in the "Introduction" to the "History of Denmark."

190 Though at this time they were greatly reduced by migrations, inundations and wars, they afterwards revived; and from this storehouse of nations came forth the Franks, Saxons, Normans, and various other tribes, which brought all Europe under Germanic sway.

renown[191]. Of their past grandeur extensive vestiges still remain, in encampments and lines on either shore[192], from the compass of which the strength and numbers of the nation may still be computed, and credit derived to the account of so prodigious an army. It was in the 640th year of Rome that the arms of the Cimbri were first heard of, under the consulate of Caecilius Metellus and Papirius Carbo; from which era to the second consulate of the emperor Trajan[193] is a period of nearly 210 years. So long has Germany withstood the arms of Rome. During this long interval many mutual wounds have been inflicted. Not the Samnite, the Carthaginian, Spain, Gaul, or Parthia, have given more frequent alarms; for the liberty of the Germans is more vigorous than the monarchy of the Arsacidae. What has the East, which has itself lost Pacorus, and suffered an overthrow from Ventidius[194], to boast against us, but the slaughter of Crassus? But the Germans, by

---

191 Their fame spread through Germany, Gaul, Spain, Britain, Italy, and as far as the Sea of Azoph (Palus Maeotis), whither, according to Posidonius, they penetrated, and called the Cimmerian or Cimbrian Bosphorus after their own name.

192 This is usually, and probably rightly, explained as relating to both shores of the Cimbric Chersonesus. Cluver and Dithmar, however, suppose that these encampments are to be sought for either in Italy, upon the river Athesis (Adige), or in Narbonnensian Gaul near Aquae Sextiae (Aix in Provence), where Florus (iii. 3) mentions that the Teutoni defeated by Marius took post in a valley with a river running through it. Of the prodigious numbers of the Cimbri who made this terrible irruption we have an account in Plutarch, who relates that their fighting men were 300,000, with a much greater number of women and children. (Plut. Marius, p. 411.)

193 Nerva was consul the fourth time, and Trajan the second, in the 851st year of Rome; in which Tacitus composed this treatise.

194 After the defeat of P. Decidius Saxa, lieutenant of Syria, by the Parthians, and the seizure of Syria by Pacorus, son of king Orodes, P. Ventidius Bassus was sent there, and vanquished the Parthians, killed Pacorus, and entirely restored the Roman affairs.

the defeat or capture of Carbo[195], Cassius[196], Scaurus Aurelius[197], Servilius Caepio, and Cneius Manlius[198], deprived the Roman

---

195 The Epitome of Livy informs us, that "in the year of Rome 640, the Cimbri, a wandering tribe, made a predatory incursion into Illyricum, where they routed the consul Papirius Carbo with his army." According to Strabo, it was at Noreia, a town of the Taurisci, near Aquileia, that Carbo was defeated. In the succeeding years, the Cimbri and Teutonia ravaged Gaul, and brought great calamities on that country; but at length, deterred by the unshaken bravery of the Gauls, they turned another way; as appears from Caesar, Bell. Gal. vii. 17. They then came into Italy, and sent ambassadors to the Senate, demanding lands to settle on. This was refused; and the consul M. Junius Silanus fought an unsuccessful battle with them, in the year of Rome 645. (Epitome of Livy, lxv.)

196 "L. Cassius the consul, in the year of Rome 647, was cut off with his army in the confines of the Allobroges, by the Tigurine Gauls, a canton of the Helvetians (now the cantons of Zurich, Appenzell, Schaffhausen, &c.), who had migrated from their settlements. The soldiers who survived the slaughter gave hostages for the payment of half they were worth, to be dismissed with safety." (Ibid.) Caesar further relates that the Roman army was passed under the yoke by the Tigurini: - "This single canton, migrating from home, within the memory of our fathers, slew the consul L. Cassius, and passed his army under the yoke." - Bell. Gall. i. 12.

197 M. Aurelius Scaurus, the consul's lieutenant (or rather consul, as he appears to have served that office in the year of Rome 646), was defeated and taken by the Cimbri; and when, being asked his advice, he dissuaded them from passing the Alps into Italy, assuring them the Romans were invincible, he was slain by a furious youth, named Boiorix. (Epit. Livy, lxvii.)

198 Florus, in like manner, considers these two affairs separately: - "Neither could Silanus sustain the first onset of the barbarians; nor Manlius, the second; nor Caepio, the third." (iii. 3.) Livy joins them together: - "By the same enemy (the Cimbri) Cn. Manlius the consul, and Q. Servilius Caepio the proconsul, were defeated in an engagement, and both dispossessed of their camps." (Epit. lxvii.) Paulus Orosius relates the affair more particularly: - "Manlius the consul, and Q. Caepio, proconsul, being sent against the Cimbri, Teutones, Tigurini, and Ambronae, Gaulish and German nations, who had conspired to extinguish the Roman empire, divided their respective provinces by the river Rhone. Here, the most violent dissensions prevailing between them, they were both overcome, to the great disgrace and danger of the Roman name. According to Antias, 80,000 Romans and allies were slaughtered. Caepio, by whose rashness this misfortune

people of five consular armies[199]; and afterwards took from Augustus himself Varus with three legions[200]. Nor did Caius Marius[201] in Italy, the deified Julius in Gaul, or Drusus, Nero,

---

was occasioned, was condemned, and his property confiscated by order of the Roman people." (Lib. v. 16.) This happened in the year of Rome 649; and the anniversary was reckoned among the unlucky days

199 The Republic; in opposition to Rome when governed by emperors.

200 This tragical catastrophe so deeply affected Augustus, that, as Seutonius informs us, "he was said to have let his beard and hair grow for several months; during which he at times struck his head against the doors, crying out, 'Varus, restore my legions!' and ever after kept the anniversary as a day of mourning." (Aug. s. 23.) The finest history piece, perhaps, ever drawn by a writer, is Tacitus's description of the army of Germanicus visiting the field of battle, six years after, and performing funeral obsequies to the scattered remains of their slaughtered countrymen. (Annals, i. 61.)

201 "After so many misfortunes, the Roman people thought no general so capable of repelling such formidable enemies, as Marius." Nor was the public opinion falsified. In his fourth consulate, in the year of Rome 652. "Marius engaged the Teutoni beyond the Alps near Aquae Sextiae (Aix in Province), killing, on the day of battle and the following day, above 150,000 of the enemy, and entirely cutting off the Teutonic nation." (Velleus Paterculus, ii. 12.) Livy says there were 200,000 slain, and 90,000 taken prisoners. The succeeding year he defeated the Cimbri, who had penetrated into Italy and crossed the Adige, in the Raudian plain, where now is Rubio, killing and taking prisoners upwards of 100,000 men. That he did not, however, obtain an unbought victory over this warlike people, may be conjectured from the resistance he met with even from their women. We are told by Florus (iii. 3) that "he was obliged to sustain an engagement with their wives, as well as themselves; who, entrenching themselves on all sides with wagons and cars, fought from them, as from towers, with lances and poles. Their death was no less glorious than their resistance. For, when they could not obtain from Marius what they requested by an embassy, their liberty, and admission into the vestal priesthood (which, indeed, could not lawfully be granted); after strangling their infants, they either fell by mutual wounds, or hung themselves on trees or the poles of their carriages in ropes made of their own hair. King Boiorix was slain, not unrevenged, fighting bravely in the field." On account of these great victories, Marius, in the year of Borne 652, triumphed over the Teutoni, Ambroni, and Cimbri.

or Germanicus[202] in their own country, defeat then without loss. The subsequent mighty threats of Caligula terminated in ridicule. Then succeeded tranquillity; till, seizing the occasion of our discords and civil wars, they forced the winter-quarters of the legions[203], and even aimed at the possession of Gaul; and, again expelled thence, they have in latter times been rather triumphed over[204] than vanquished.

38. We have now to speak of the Suevi[205]; who do not compose a single state, like the Catti or Tencteri, but occupy the greatest part of Germany, and are still distributed into different names and nations, although all hearing the common appellation of Suevi. It is a characteristic of this people to turn their hair sideways, and tie it beneath the poll in a knot. By this mark the Suevi are distinguished from the rest of the Germans; and the freemen of the Suevi from the slaves[206]. Among other nations, this mode, either

---

202 In the 596th year of Rome, Julius Caesar defeated Ariovistus, a German king, near Dampierre in the Franche-Comte, and pursued his routed troops with great slaughter thirty miles towards the Rhine, filling all that space with spoils and dead bodies. (Bell. Gall. i. 33 and 52.) He had before chastised the Tigurini, who, as already mentioned, had defeated and killed L. Cassius. Drusus: This was the son of Livia, and brother of the emperor Tiberius. He was in Germany B.C. 12, 11. His loss was principally from shipwreck on the coast of the Chauci. See Lynam's Roman Emperors, i. 37, 45, Nero; i.e. Tiberius, afterwards emperor. His name was Tiberius Claudius Drusus Nero. See Lynam's Roman Emperors, i. 51, 53, 62, 78. Germanicus: He was the son of Drusus, and so nephew of Tiberius. His victories in Germany took place A.D. 14-16. He too, like his father, was shipwrecked, and nearly at the same spot. See Lynam's Roman Emperors, i. 103-118.

203 In the war of Civilis, related by Tacitus, Hist. iv. and v.

204 By Domitian, as is more particularly mentioned in the Life of Agricola.

205 The Suevi possessed that extensive tract of country lying between the Elbe, the Vistula, the Baltic Sea, and the Danube. They formerly had spread still further, reaching even to the Rhine. Hence Strabo, Caesar, Florus, and others, have referred to the Suevi what related to the Catti.

206 Among the Suevi, and also the rest of the Germans, the slaves, seem to

on account of some relationship with the Suevi, or from the usual propensity to imitation, is sometimes adopted; but rarely, and only during the period of youth. The Suevi, even till they are hoary, continue to have their hair growing stiffly backwards, and often it is fastened on the very crown of the head. The chiefs dress it with still greater care: and in this respect they study ornament, though of an undebasing kind. For their design is not to make love, or inspire it; they decorate themselves in this manner as they proceed to war, in order to seem taller and more terrible; and dress for the eyes of their enemies.

39. The Semnones[207] assert themselves to be the most ancient and noble of the Suevi; and their pretensions are confirmed by religion. At a stated time, all the people of the same lineage assemble by their delegates in a wood, consecrated by the auguries of their forefathers and ancient terror, and there by the public slaughter of a human victim celebrate the horrid origin of their barbarous rites. Another kind of reverence is paid to the grove. No person enters it without being bound with a chain, as an acknowledgment of his inferior nature, and the power of the deity residing there. If he accidentally fall, it is not lawful for him to be lifted or to rise up; they roll themselves out along the ground. The whole of their superstition has this import: that from this spot the nation derives its origin; that here is the residence of the Deity, the Governor of all, and that everything else is subject and subordinate to him. These opinions receive additional authority from the power of the Semnones, who inhabit a hundred cantons, and, from the great body they compose, consider themselves as the head of the Suevi.

40. The Langobardi[208], on the other hand, are ennobled by, the

---

have been shaven; or at least cropped so short that they could not twist or tie up their hair in a knot.

207 The Semnones inhabited both banks of the Viadrus (Oder); the country which is now part of Pomerania, of the Marche of Brandenburg, and of Lusatia.

208 In the reign of Augustus, the Langobardi dwelt on this side the Elbe,

smallness of their numbers; since though surrounded by many powerful nations, they derive security, not from obsequiousness, but from their martial enterprise. The neighboring Reudigni[209], and the Avions[210], Angli[211], Varini, Eudoses, Suardones, and Nuithones[212], are defended by rivers or forests. Nothing remarkable occurs in any of these; except that they unite in the worship of Hertha[213],

---

between Luneburg and Magdeburg. When conquered and driven beyond the Elbe by Tiberius, they occupied that part of the country where are now Prignitz, Ruppin, and part of the Middle Marche. They afterwards founded the Lombard kingdom in Italy; which, in the year of Christ 774, was destroyed by Charlemagne, who took their king Desiderius, and subdued all Italy. The laws of the Langobardi are still extant, and may be met with in Lindenbrog. The Burgundians are not mentioned by Tacitus, probably because they were then an inconsiderable people. Afterwards, joining with the Langobardi, they settled on the Decuman lands and the Roman boundary. They from thence made an irruption into Gaul, and seized that country which is still named from them Burgundy. Their laws are likewise extant.

209 From Tacitus's description, the Reudigni must have dwelt in part of the present duchy of Mecklenburg, and of Lauenburg. They had formerly been settled on this side the Elbe, on the sands of Luneburg.

210 Perhaps the same people with those called by Mamertinus, in his Panegyric on Maximian, the Chaibones. From their vicinity to the fore- mentioned nations, they must have inhabited part of the duchy of Mecklenburg. They had formerly dwelt on this side the Elbe, on the banks of the river Ilmenavia in Luneburg; which is now called Ava; whence, probably, the name of the people.

211 Inhabitants of what is now part of Holstein and Sleswig; in which tract is still a district called Angeln, between Flensborg and Sleswig. In the fifth century, the Angles, in conjunction with the Saxons, migrated into Britain, and perpetuated their name by giving appellation to England.

212 From the enumeration of Tacitus, and the situation of the other tribes, it appears that the Eudoses must have occupied the modern Wismar and Rostock; the Suardones, Stralsund, Swedish Pomerania, and part of the Hither Pomerania, and of the Uckerane Marche. Eccard, however, supposes these nations were much more widely extended; and that the Eudoses dwelt upon the Oder; the Suardones, upon the Warte; the Nuithones, upon the Netze.

213 The ancient name of the goddess Herth still subsists in the German Erde, and in the English Earth.

or Mother Earth; and suppose her to interfere in the affairs of men, and to visit the different nations. In an island[214] of the ocean stands a sacred and unviolated grove, in which is a consecrated chariot, covered with a veil, which the priest alone is permitted to touch. He becomes conscious of the entrance of the goddess into this secret recess; and with profound veneration attends the vehicle, which is drawn by yoked cows. At this season[215], all is joy; and every place which the goddess deigns to visit is a scene of festivity. No wars are undertaken; arms are untouched; and every hostile weapon is shut up. Peace abroad and at home are then only known; then only loved; till at length the same priest reconducts the goddess, satiated with mortal intercourse, to her temple[216]. The chariot, with its curtain, and, if we may believe it, the goddess herself, then undergo ablution in a secret lake. This office is performed by slaves, whom the same lake instantly swallows up. Hence proceeds a mysterious horror; and a holy ignorance of what that can be, which is beheld only by those who are about to perish. This part of the Suevian nation extends to the most remote recesses of Germany.

41. If we now follow the course of the Danube, as we before did

---

214 Many suppose this island to have been the isle of Rugen in the Baltic sea. It is more probable, however, that it was an island near the mouth of the Elbe, now called the isle of Helgeland, or Heiligeland (Holy Island). Besides the proof arising from the name, the situation agrees better with that of the nations before enumerated.

215 Olaus Rudbeck contends that this festival was celebrated in winter, and still continues in Scandinavia under the appellation of Julifred, the peace of Juul. (Yule is the term used for Christmas season in the old English and Scottish dialects.) But this feast was solemnized not in honor of the Earth, but of the Sun, called by them Thor or Taranium. The festival of Herth was held later, in the month of February; as may be seen in Mallet's "Introduction to the History of Denmark."

216 Templo here means merely "the consecrated place," i.e. the grove before mentioned, for according to c.9 the Germans built no temples.

that of the Rhine, we first meet with the Hermunduri[217]; a people faithful to the Romans[218], and on that account the only Germans who are admitted to commerce, not on the bank alone, but within our territories, and in the flourishing colony[219] established in the province of Rhaetia. They pass and repass at pleasure, without being attended by a guard; and while we exhibit to other nations our arms and camps alone, to these we lay open our houses and country seats, which they behold without coveting. In the country of the Hermunduri rises the Elbe[220]; a river formerly celebrated and known among us, now only heard of by name.

42. Contiguous to the Hermunduri are the Narisci[221]; and next to

---

217 It is supposed that this people, on account of their valor, were called Heermanner; corrupted by the Romans into Hermunduri. They were first settled between the Elbe, the Sala, and Bohemia; where now are Anhalt, Voightland, Saxony, part of Misnia, and of Franconia. Afterwards, when the Marcomanni took possession of Bohemia, from which the Boii had been expelled by Maroboduus, the Hermunduri added their settlements to their own, and planted in them the Suevian name, whence is derived the modern appellation of that country, Suabia.

218 They were so at that time; but afterwards joined with the Marcomanni and other Germans against the Romans in the time of Marcus Aurelius, who overcame them.

219 Augusta Vindelicorum, now Augsburg; a famous Roman colony in the province of Rhaetia, of which Vindelica was then a part.

220 Tacitus is greatly mistaken if he confounds the source of the Egra, which is in the country of the Hermuduri, with that of the Elbe, which rises in Bohemia. The Elbe had been formerly, as Tacitus observes, well known to the Romans by the victories of Drusus, Tiberius, and Domitius; but afterwards, when the increasing power of the Germans kept the Roman arms at a distance, it was only indistinctly heard of. Hence its source was probably inaccurately laid down in the Roman geographical tables. Perhaps, however, the Hermunduri, when they had served in the army of Maroboduus, received lands in that part of Bohemia in which the Elbe rises; in which case there would be no mistake in Tacitus's account.

221 Inhabitants of that part of Bavaria which lies between Bohemia and the Danube.

them, the Marcomanni[222] and Quadi[223]. Of these, the Marcomanni are the most powerful and renowned; and have even acquired the country which they inhabit, by their valor in expelling the Boii[224]. Nor are the Narisci and Quadi inferior in bravery[225]; and this is, as it were, the van of Germany as far as it is bordered by the Danube. Within our memory the Marcomanni and Quadi were governed by kings of their own nation, of the noble line of Maroboduus[226] and Tudrus. They now submit even to foreigners; but all the power of their kings depends upon the authority of the Romans[227]. We seldom assist them with our arms, but frequently with our money; nor are they the less potent on that account.

---

222 Inhabitants of Bohemia.

223 Inhabitants of Moravia, and the part of Austria between it and the Danube. Of this people, Ammianus Marcellinus, in his account of the reign of Valentinian and Valens, thus speaks: - "A sudden commotion arose among the Quadi; a nation at present of little consequence, but which was formerly extremely warlike and potent, as their exploits sufficiently evince." - xxix. 15.

224 Their expulsion of the Boii, who had given name to Bohemia, has been already mentioned. Before this period, the Marcomanni dwelt near the sources of the Danube, where now is the duchy of Wirtemburg; and, as Dithmar supposes, on account of their inhabiting the borders of Germany, were called Marcmanner, from Marc (the same with the old English March) a border, or boundary.

225 These people justified their military reputation by the dangerous war which, in conjunction with the Marcomanni, they excited against the Romans, in the reign of Marcus Aurelius.

226 Of this prince, and his alliance with the Romans against Arminius, mention is made by Tacitus, Annals, ii.

227 Thus Vannius was made king of the Quadi by Tiberius. (See Annals, ii. 63.) At a later period, Antoninus Pius (as appears from a medal preserved in Spanheim) gave them Furtius for their king. And when they had expelled him, and set Ariogaesus on the throne, Marcus Aurelius, to whom he was obnoxious, refused to confirm the election. (Dio, lxxi.)

43. Behind these are the Marsigni[228], Gothini[229], Osi[230], and Burrii[231], who close the rear of the Marcomanni and Quadi. Of these, the Marsigni and Burrii in language[232] and dress resemble the Suevi. The Gothini and Osi prove themselves not to be Germans; the first, by their use of the Gallic, the second, of the Pannonian tongue; and both, by their submitting to pay tribute: which is levied on them, as aliens, partly by the Sarmatians, partly by the Quadi. The Gothini, to their additional disgrace, work iron mines[233]. All these people inhabit but a small proportion of champaign country; their settlements are chiefly amongst forests, and on the sides and summits of mountains; for a continued ridge of mountains[234] separates Suevia from various remoter tribes. Of these, the Lygian [235] is the most extensive, and diffuses its name through several communities. It will be sufficient to name the most powerful of

---

228 These people inhabited what is now Galatz, Jagerndorf, and part of Silesia.

229 Inhabitants of part of Silesia, and of Hungary.

230 Inhabitants of part of Hungary to the Danube.

231 These were settled about the Carpathian mountains, and the sources of the Vistula.

232 It is probable that the Suevi were distinguished from the rest of the Germans by a peculiar dialect, as well as by their dress and manners.

233 Ptolemy mentions iron mines in or near the country of the Quadi. I should imagine that the expression "additional disgrace" (or, more literally, "which might make them more ashamed") does not refer merely to the slavery of working in mines, but to the circumstance of their digging up iron, the substance by means of which they might acquire freedom and independence. This is quite in the manner of Tacitus. The word iron was figuratively used by the ancients to signify military force in general. Thus Solon, in his well-known answer to Croesus, observed to him, that the nation which possessed more iron would be master of all his gold. - Aikin.

234 The mountains between Moravia, Hungary, Silesia, and Bohemia.

235 The Lygii inhabited what is now part of Silesia, of the New Marche, of Prussia and Poland on this side the Vistula.

them - the Arii, Helvecones, Manimi, Elysii, and Naharvali[236]. In the country of the latter is a grove, consecrated to religious rites of great antiquity. A priest presides over them, dressed in woman's apparel; but the gods worshipped there are said, according to the Roman interpretation, to be Castor and Pollux. Their attributes are the same; their name, Alcis[237]. No images, indeed, or vestiges of foreign superstition, appear in their worship; but they are revered under the character of young men and brothers. The Arii, fierce beyond the superiority of strength they possess over the other just enumerated people, improve their natural ferocity of aspect by artificial helps. Their shields are black; their bodies painted[238]: they choose the darkest nights for an attack; and strike terror by the funereal gloom of their sable bands - no enemy being able to sustain their singular, and, as it were, infernal appearance; since in every combat the eyes are the first part subdued. Beyond the Lygii are the Gothones[239], who live under a monarchy, somewhat more strict than that of the other German nations, yet not to a

---

236 These tribes were settled between the Oder and Vistula, where now are part of Silesia, of Brandenburg, and of Poland. The Elysii are supposed to have given name to Silesia.

237 The Greeks and Romans, under the name of the Dioscuri, or Castor and Pollux, worshipped those meteorous exhalations which, during a storm, appear on the masts of ships, and are supposed to denote an approaching calm. A kind of religious veneration is still paid to this phenomenon by the Roman Catholics, under the appellation of the fire of St. Elmo. The Naharvali seem to have affixed the same character of divinity on the ignis fatuus; and the name Alcis is probably the same with that of Alff or Alp, which the northern nations still apply to the fancied Genii of the mountains. The Sarmatian deities Lebus and Polebus, the memory of whom still subsists in the Polish festivals, had, perhaps, the same origin.

238 No custom has been more universal among uncivilized people than painting the body, either for the purpose of ornament, or that of inspiring terror.

239 Inhabitants of what is now Further Pomerania, the New Marche and the Western part of Poland, between the Oder and Vistula. They were a different people from the Goths, though, perhaps, in alliance with them.

degree incompatible with liberty. Adjoining to these are the Rugii[240] and Lemovii[241], situated on the sea-coast - all these tribes are distinguished by round shields, short swords, and submission to regal authority.

44. Next occur the communities of the Suiones[242], seated in the very Ocean[243], who, besides their strength in men and arms, also possess a naval force[244]. The form of their vessels differs from ours in having a prow at each end[245], so that they are always ready

---

240 These people were settled on the shore of the Baltic, where now are Colburg, Cassubia, and Further Pomerania. Their name is still preserved in the town of Rugenwald and Isle of Rugen.

241 These were also settlers on the Baltic, about the modern Stolpe, Dantzig, and Lauenburg. The Heruli appear afterwards to have occupied the settlements of the Lemovii. Of these last no further mention occurs; but the Heruli made themselves famous throughout Europe and Asia, and were the first of the Germans who founded a kingdom in Italy under Odoacer.

242 The Suiones inhabited Sweden, and the Danish isles of Funen, Langlaud, Zeeland, Laland, &c. From them and the Cimbri were derived the Normans, who, after spreading terror through various parts of the empire, at last seized upon the fertile province of Normandy in France. The names of Goths, Visigoths, and Ostrogoths, became still more famous, they being the nations who accomplished the ruin of the Roman empire. The laws of the Visigoths are still extant; but they depart much from the usual simplicity of the German laws.

243 The Romans, who had but an imperfect knowledge of this part of the world, imagined here those "vast insular tracts" mentioned in the beginning of this treatise. Hence Pliny, also, says of the Baltic sea (Codanus sinus), that "it is filled with islands, the most famous of which, Scandinavia (now Sweden and Norway), is of an undiscovered magnitude; that part of it only being known which is occupied by the Hilleviones, a nation inhabiting five hundred cantons; who call this country another globe." (Lib. iv. 13.) The memory of the Hilleviones is still preserved in the part of Sweden named Halland.

244 Their naval power continued so great, that they had the glory of framing the nautical code, the laws of which were first written at Wisby, the capital of the isle of Gothland, in the eleventh century.

245 This is exactly the form of the Indian canoes, which, however, are generally worked with sails as well as oars.

to advance. They make no use of sails, nor have regular benches of oars at the sides: they row, as is practised in some rivers, without order, sometimes on one side, sometimes on the other, as occasion requires. These people honor wealth[246]; for which reason they are subject to monarchical government, without any limitations[247], or precarious conditions of allegiance. Nor are arms allowed to be kept promiscuously, as among the other German nations: but are committed to the charge of a keeper, and he, too, a slave. The pretext is, that the Ocean defends them from any sudden incursions; and men unemployed, with arms in their hands, readily become licentious. In fact, it is for the king's interest not to entrust a noble, a freeman, or even an emancipated slave, with the custody of arms.

45. Beyond the Suiones is another sea, sluggish and almost stagnant[248], by which the whole globe is imagined to be girt and enclosed, from this circumstance, that the last light of the setting sun continues so vivid till its rising, as to obscure the stars[249]. Popular

---

246 The great opulence of a temple of the Suiones, as described by Adam of Bremen (Eccl. Hist. ch. 233), is a proof of the wealth that at all times has attended naval dominion. "This nation," says he, "possesses a temple of great renown, called Ubsola (now Upsal), not far from the cities Sictona and Birca (now Sigtuna and Bioerkoe). In this temple, which is entirely ornamented with gold, the people worship the statues of three gods; the most powerful of whom, Thor, is seated on a couch in the middle; with Woden on one side, and Fricca on the other." From the ruins of the towns Sictona and Birca arose the present capital of Sweden, Stockholm.

247 Hence Spener (Notit. German. Antiq.) rightly concludes that the crown was hereditary, and not elective, among the Suiones.

248 It is uncertain whether what is now called the Frozen Ocean is here meant, or the northern extremities of the Baltic Sea, the Gulfs of Bothnia and Finland, which are so frozen every winter as to be unnavigable.

249 The true principles of astronomy have now taught us the reason why, at a certain latitude, the sun, at the summer solstice, appears never to set: and at a lower latitude, the evening twilight continues till morning.

belief adds, that the sound of his emerging[250] from the ocean is also heard; and the forms of deities[251], with the rays beaming from his head, are beheld. Only thus far, report says truly, does nature extend[252]. On the right shore of the Suevic sea[253] dwell the tribes of the Aestii[254], whose dress and customs are the same with those of the Suevi, but their language more resembles the British[255]. They worship the mother of the gods[256]; and as the symbol of their superstition, they carry about them the figures of wild boars[257]. This serves them in place of armor and every other defence: it renders the votary of the goddess safe even in the midst of foes. Their weapons are chiefly clubs, iron being little used among

---

250 The true reading here is, probably, "immerging;" since it was a common notion at that period, that the descent of the sun into the ocean was attended with a kind of hissing noise, like red hot iron dipped into water. Thus Juvenal, Sat. xiv, 280: -

Audiet Herculeo stridentem gurgite solem.

"Hear the sun hiss in the Herculean gulf."

251 Instead of formas deorum, "forms of deities," some, with more probability, read equorum, "of the horses," which are feigned to draw the chariot of the sun.

252 Thus Quintus Curtius, speaking of the Indian Ocean, says, "Nature itself can proceed no further."

253 The Baltic Sea.

254 Now, the kingdom of Prussia, the duchies of Samogitia and Courland, the palatinates of Livonia and Esthonia, in the name of which last the ancient appellation of these people is preserved.

255 Because the inhabitants of this extreme part of Germany retained the Scythico-Celtic language, which long prevailed in Britain.

256 A deity of Scythian origin, called Frea or Fricca. See Mallet's Introduct. to Hist. of Denmark.

257 Many vestiges of this superstition remain to this day in Sweden. The peasants, in the month of February, the season formerly sacred to Frea, make little images of boars in paste, which they apply to various superstitious uses. (See Eccard.) A figure of a Mater Deum, with the boar, is given by Mr. Pennant, in his Tour in Scotland, 1769, p. 268, engraven from a stone found at the great station at Netherby in Cumberland.

them. They cultivate corn and other fruits of the earth with more industry than German indolence commonly exerts[258]. They even explore the sea; and are the only people who gather amber, which by them is called Glese[259], and is collected among the shallows and upon the shore[260]. With the usual indifference of barbarians, they have not inquired or ascertained from what natural object or by what means it is produced. It long lay disregarded[261] amidst other things thrown up by the sea, till our luxury[262] gave it a name. Useless to them, they gather it in the rough; bring it unwrought; and wonder at the price they receive. It would appear, however, to be an exudation from certain trees; since reptiles, and even winged animals, are often seen shining through it, which, entangled in it while in a liquid state, became enclosed as it hardened[263]. I should

---

258 The cause of this was, probably, their confined situation, which did not permit them to wander in hunting and plundering parties, like the rest of the Germans.

259 This name was transferred to glass when it came into use. Pliny speaks of the production of amber in this country as follows: - "It is certain that amber is produced in the islands of the Northern Ocean, and is called by the Germans gless. One of these islands, by the natives named Austravia, was on this account called Glessaria by our sailors in the fleet of Germanicus." - Lib. xxxvii. 3.

260 Much of the Prussian amber is even at present collected on the shores of the Baltic. Much also is found washed out of the clayey cliffs of Holderness. See Tour in Scotland, 1769, p. 16.

261 Insomuch that the Guttones, who formerly inhabited this coast, made use of amber as fuel, and sold it for that purpose to the neighboring Teutones. (Plin. xxxvii. 2.)

262 Various toys and utensils of amber, such as bracelets, necklaces, rings, cups, and even pillars, were to be met with among the luxurious Romans.

263 In a work by Goeppert and Berendt, on "Amber and the Fossil Remains of Plants contained in it," published at Berlin, 1845, a passage is found (of which a translation is here given) which quite harmonizes with the account of Tacitus: - "About the parts which are known by the name of Samland an island emerged, or rather a group of islands, ... which gradually increased in circumference, and, favored by a mild sea climate, was overspread with vegetation and forest.

therefore imagine that, as the luxuriant woods and groves in the secret recesses of the East exude frankincense and balsam, so there are the same in the islands and continents of the West; which, acted upon by the near rays of the sun, drop their liquid juices into the subjacent sea, whence, by the force of tempests, they are thrown out upon the opposite coasts. If the nature of amber be examined by the application of fire, it kindles like a torch, with a thick and odorous flame; and presently resolves into a glutinous matter resembling pitch or resin. The several communities of the Sitones[264] succeed those of the Suiones; to whom they are similar in other respects, but differ in submitting to a female reign; so far have they degenerated, not only from liberty, but even from slavery. Here Suevia terminates.

46. I am in doubt whether to reckon the Peucini, Venedi, and Fenni among the Germans or Sarmatians[265]; although the Peucini[266], who are by some called Bastarnae, agree with the Germans in language, apparel, and habitations[267]. All of them live in filth and

---

This forest was the means of amber being produced. Certain trees in it exuded gums in such quantities that the sunken forest soil now appears to be filled with it to such a degree, as if it had only been deprived of a very trifling part of its contents by the later eruptions of the sea, and the countless storms which have lashed the ocean for centuries." Hence, though found underground, it appears to have been originally the production of some resinous tree. Hence, too, the reason of the appearance of insects, &c. in it, as mentioned by Tacitus.

264 Norwegians.

265 All beyond the Vistula was reckoned Sarmatia. These people, therefore, were properly inhabitants of Sarmatia, though from their manners they appeared of German origin.

266 Pliny also reckons the Peucini among the German nations: - "The fifth part of Germany is possessed by the Peucini and Bastarnae, who border on the Dacians." (iv. 14.) From Strabo it appears that the Peucini, part of the Bastarnae, inhabited the country about the mouths of the Danube, and particularly the island Peuce, now Piczina, formed by the river.

267 The habitations of the Peucini were fixed; whereas the Sarmatians wandered about in their wagons.

laziness. The intermarriages of their chiefs with the Sarmatians have debased them by a mixture of the manners of that people[268]. The Venedi have drawn much from this source[269]; for they overrun in their predatory excursions all the woody and mountainous tracts between the Peucini and Fenni. Yet even these are rather to be referred to the Germans, since they build houses, carry shields, and travel with speed on foot; in all which particulars they totally differ from the Sarmatians, who pass their time in wagons and on horseback[270]. The Fenni[271] live in a state of amazing savageness and squalid poverty. They are destitute of arms, horses, and settled

---

268 "Sordes omnium ac torpor; procerum connubiis mixtis nonnihil in Sarmatarum habitum foedantur." In many editions the semicolon is placed not after torpor, but after procerum. The sense of the passage so read is: "The chief men are lazy and stupid, besides being filthy, like all the rest. Intermarriage with the Sarmatians have debased." &c.

269 The Venedi extended beyond the Peucini and Bastarnae as far as the Baltic Sea; where is the Sinus Venedicus, now the Gulf of Dantzig. Their name is also preserved in Wenden, a part of Livonia. When the German nations made their irruption into Italy, France and Spain, the Venedi, also called Winedi, occupied their vacant settlements between the Vistula and Elbe. Afterwards they crossed the Danube, and seized Dalmatia, Illyricum, Istria, Carniola, and the Noric Alps. A part of Carniola still retains the name of Windismarck, derived from them. This people were also called Slavi; and their language, the Sclavonian, still prevails through a vast tract of country.

270 This is still the manner of living of the successors of the Sarmatians, the Nogai Tartars.

271 Their country is called by Pliny, Eningia, now Finland. Warnefrid (De Gest. Langobard. i. 5) thus describes their savage and wretched state: - "The Scritobini, or Scritofinni, are not without snow in the midst of summer; and, being little superior in sagacity to the brutes, live upon no other food than the raw flesh of wild animals, the hairy skins of which they use for clothing. They derive their name, according to the barbarian tongue, from leaping, because they hunt wild beasts by a certain method of leaping or springing with pieces of wood bent in the shape of a bow." Here is an evident description of the snow-shoes or raquets in common use among the North American savages, as well as the inhabitants of the most northern parts of Europe.

abodes: their food is herbs[272]; their clothing, skins; their bed, the ground. Their only dependence is on their arrows, which, for want of iron, are headed with bone[273]; and the chase is the support of the women as well as the men; the former accompany the latter in the pursuit, and claim a share of the prey. Nor do they provide any other shelter for their infants from wild beasts and storms, than a covering of branches twisted together. This is the resort of youth; this is the receptacle of old age. Yet even this way of life is in their estimation happier than groaning over the plough; toiling in the erection of houses; subjecting their own fortunes and those of others to the agitations of alternate hope and fear. Secure against men, secure against the gods, they have attained the most difficult point, not to need even a wish.

All our further accounts are intermixed with fable; as, that the Hellusii and Oxionae[274] have human faces, with the bodies and limbs of wild beasts. These unauthenticated reports I shall leave untouched[275].

---

272 As it is just after mentioned that their chief dependence is on the game procured in hunting, this can only mean that the vegetable food they use consists of wild herbs, in opposition to the cultivated products of the earth.

273 The Esquimaux and the South Sea islanders do the same thing to this day.

274 People of Lapland. The origin of this fable was probably the manner of clothing in these cold regions, where the inhabitants bury themselves in the thickest furs, scarcely leaving anything of the form of a human creature.

275 It is with true judgment that this excellent historian forbears to intermix fabulous narrations with the interesting and instructive matter of this treatise. Such a mixture might have brought an impeachment on the fidelity of the account in general; which, notwithstanding the suspicions professed by some critics, contains nothing but what is entirely consonant to truth and nature. Had Tacitus indulged his invention in the description of German manners, is it probable that he could have given so just a picture of the state of a people under similar circumstances, the savage tribes of North America, as we have seen them within the present century? As long as the original constitution and jurisprudence of our own and other European countries are studied, this treatise will be regarded as one of the most precious and authentic monuments of historical antiquity.

ABOUT CODA BOOKS

Most Coda books are edited and endorsed by Emmy Award winning film maker and military historian Bob Carruthers, producer of Discovery Channel's Line of Fire and Weapons of War and BBC's Both Sides of the Line. Long experience and strong editorial control gives the military history enthusiast the ability to buy with confidence.

The series advisor is David McWhinnie, producer of the acclaimed Battlefield series for Discovery Channel. David and Bob have co-produced books and films with a wide variety of the UK's leading historians including Professor John Erickson and Dr David Chandler.

Where possible the books draw on rare primary sources to give the military enthusiast new insights into a fascinating subject.

www.codabooks.com

The English Civil Wars

The Zulu Wars

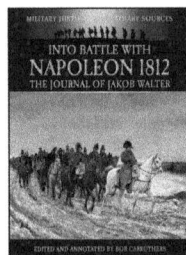

Into Battle with Napoleon 1812

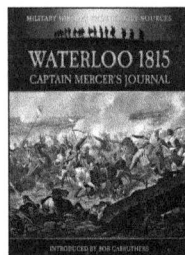

Waterloo 1815

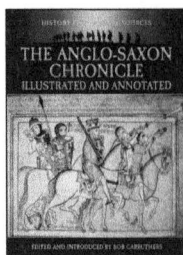

The Anglo-Saxon Chronicle

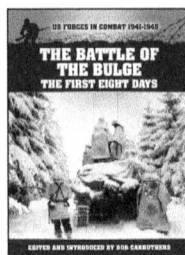

The Battle of the Bulge

The Normandy Campaign 1944

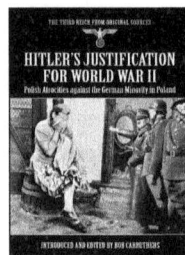

Hitler's Justification for WWII

Hitler's Mein Kampf -
The Roots of Evil

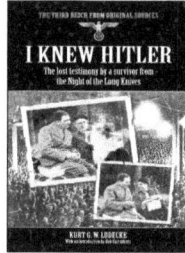
I Knew Hitler

Mein Kampf - The 1939
Illustrated Edition

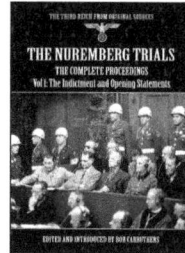
The Nuremberg Trials Volume 1

Tiger I in Combat

Tiger I Crew Manual

Panzers at War 1939-1942

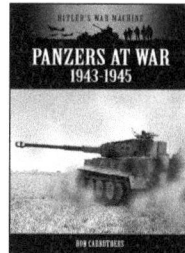
Panzers at War 1943-1945

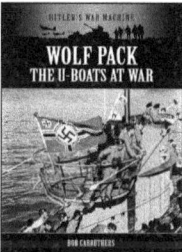
Wolf Pack - the U boats

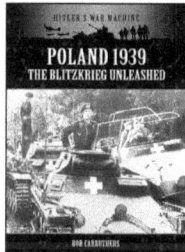
Poland 1939

Luftwaffe Combat Reports

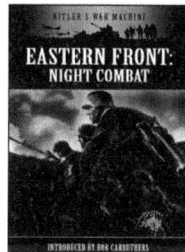
Eastern Front Night Combat

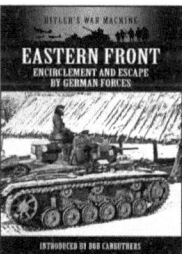
Eastern Front Encirclement

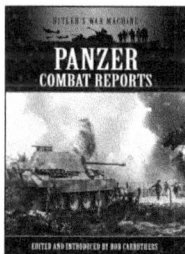
Panzer Combat Reports

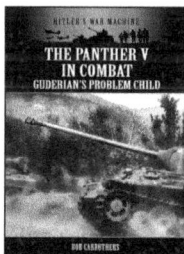
The Panther V in Combat

The Red Army in Combat

Barbarossa - Hitler Turns East

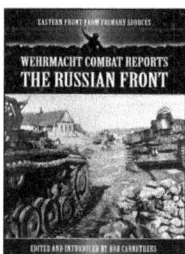
The Russian Front

The Wehrmacht in Russia

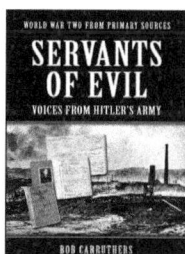
Servants of Evil

Milton Keynes UK
Ingram Content Group UK Ltd.
UKHW020635110124
435856UK00009B/278